THE LITTLE BOOK OF DELPHI

HUW COLLINGBOURNE

bitwise books

The Little Book Of Delphi

ISBN: 978-1-913132-09-5

bitwise books is an imprint of **dark neon ltd.**

written by
Huw Collingbourne

DOWNLOAD THE SOURCE CODE

All the source code of the examples in this book may be downloaded (free) from the publisher's web site:
http://www.bitwisebooks.com/

Contents

Introduction

Welcome to *The Little Book Of Delphi Programming.* In the next ten chapters, I will guide you through the basics of writing computer programs using the Object Pascal language.

The aim of this book is to teach you to use Delphi to design and program applications in the Object Pascal language. There are lots of short sample programs in this books and you can download the full source code of these from the Bitwise Books web site.

What is Delphi?

The Delphi integrated development environment (IDE) provides a drag-and-drop designer which makes it simple to create user interfaces and 'attach' Object Pascal code to events such as button-clicks. The name Delphi is used to describe the IDE and its associated tools while the programming language is termed Object Pascal. Delphi was originally developed by the Borland company in 1995. It is now owned by Embarcadero Technologies.

Download the Source Code

The source code is provided with this course in the form of a downloadable Zip archive from the Bitwise Books web site: http://www.bitwisebooks.com

What is in this Book?

This book will teach you to program in the Object Pascal language with Delphi. It explains the fundamental features of the language then moves on to more demanding topics: everything from Object Pascal's object orientation to file-handling, exception-handling and streaming. Each of the books in *Little Book* series aims to give you *just the stuff you really need* to get straight to the heart of the matter without all the fluff and padding.

What is not in this Book

This book does not deal with 'special types' of Delphi program such as database applications or cross-platform applications. It does not cover in any detail Object Pascal programming with other compilers or IDEs such as Free Pascal and Lazarus. Not does it provide 'reference documentation' for Delphi's units, classes and methods. All these topics are well documented online (see the Appendix). The sole purpose of this book is to teach the Object Pascal language with Delphi.

Who Should Read this Book?

This book is suitable for both beginners and more experienced programmers switching to Object Pascal from some other language such as C#, Java, Ruby or Python. While Object Pascal can be used on different programming platforms (using tools such as Lazarus and Free Pascal), Delphi runs on Windows. This book assumes, therefore, that you will program Object Pascal using Delphi on Windows. The aim of the book is to teach how to program Object Pascal with Delphi. It is mainly about the language itself rather than about developing specific types of application. If you are a Windows programmer who needs a quick way to learn to program Object Pascal with Delphi, this book is for you.

How To Read This Book

If you are a **beginner programmer**, I recommend that you read every chapter in order and be sure to try out all the sample projects from the code archive.

If **you can already program in another language**, feel free to skip some of the explanations of fundamental programming features (explanations of variables, types and so on) but be sure that you understand Pascal syntax (for example, its use of keywords instead of the curly braces you may be familiar with from C or Java, and Pascal's distinction between procedures and functions).

Experienced programmers may want to jump into chapters out of sequence. All the sample programs are small and self-contained so you can pick and choose which topics and projects to study first.

Making Sense of the Text

In **The Little Book Of Delphi**, any Pascal source code is written like this:

```
procedure ShowGreeting;
begin
    Memo1.Lines.Add('Hello World');
end;
```

When there is a sample program to accompany the code, the program name is shown above the code, like this:

helloworld

```
procedure ShowGreeting;
begin
    Memo1.Lines.Add('Hello World');
end;
```

To load a named program from the code archive you will need to load the Delphi project ending with *dpr* – so, to load the *helloworld* program you would need to load the *helloworld.dpr* project.

Any output that you may expect to see when a program is run is shown like this:

```
Hello World!
```

Explanatory notes (which generally provide some hints or give a more in-depth explanation of some point mentioned in the text) are shown like this:

This Is A Note

This is an explanatory note. You can skip it if you like – but if you do so, you may miss something of interest…!

What is Lazarus?

Delphi is the de facto standard environment for creating Object Pascal applications and this book assumes that you will be using Delphi. The Delphi IDE runs on Windows only. If you want to create Object Pascal applications on macOS or Linux, you can use the Lazarus development environment with the Free Pascal compiler.

The Free Pascal compiler is available for multiple platforms including Windows, macOS and Linux. Just like Delphi, Lazarus can create visual user interfaces, add code, and compile, run or debug applications all within an integrated environment. While most of the code in this book should compile and run without error with Lazarus, this is not guaranteed and the book provides no specific support for Lazarus or Free Pascal. See the Appendix for more on Lazarus and Free Pascal.

About the Author

Huw Collingbourne has been programming in Pascal since the early 1980s. He is the author of the cult text adventure game, *The Golden Wombat Of Destiny* (which was written in Turbo Pascal). He is an online programming instructor with successful courses on Delphi and Object Pascal, C, C#, Java and other programming languages and topics. For a full list of available courses go to the Bitwise Courses web site: http://bitwisecourses.com/
Huw is author of *The Little Book Of C#*, *The Little Book Of Ruby*, *The Little Book Of C*, *The Little Book Of Pointers* and *The Little Book Of Recursion* from Bitwise Books. He is a well-known technology writer in the UK and has written numerous opinion and programming columns for a number of computer magazines, such as Computer Shopper, PC Pro, and PC Plus. He wrote the Delphi programming column in PC Plus for over ten years. At various times Huw has been a magazine publisher, editor, and TV broadcaster. He has an MA in English from the University of Cambridge and holds a 2nd dan black belt in aikido, a martial art which he teaches in North Devon, UK.

About the Technical Editor

Dr. Dermot Hogan is a software developer who has led major projects written in Assembly Language, C , C# and a number of other programming languages. A specialist in real time trading technologies, he has managed and developed global risk management systems for several international banks and financial institutions. He is the lead developer of the independent software company, SapphireSteel Software. He holds a Ph.D in physics from the University of Cambridge. His current area of research is devoted to robotic control and imaging systems.

Chapter 1 – Getting Started

This chapter explains what you need to do in order to get started with Object Pascal programming using Delphi and the source code archive that accompanies this book.

In order to write Object Pascal programs you need an editor, a compiler (the tool that translates the code you write into a runnable program) and a set of other tools to design and build your applications. Delphi provides an integrated environment for designing, coding, compiling and debugging Object Pascal applications. Before going any further, you will need to install Delphi on your PC.

Install Delphi

You may either use a commercial edition of Delphi or the free 'Community' edition. The Community edition has most of the same features as the commercial editions including the code editor, visual designer and integrated debugger. Delphi may be Downloaded from Embarcadero here: https://www.embarcadero.com/

What is RAD Studio?

Delphi is also integrated into Embarcadero's RAD Studio IDE. This is a commercial RAD (Rapid Application Development) product which supports both Object Pascal and C++ development into a single environment. The programs in this book are compatible with RAD Studio as well as with the free edition of Delphi. The screenshots all show Delphi. Some menu items and dialogs may be slightly different in RAD Studio.

Delphi Overview

This screenshot identifies some important elements of the Delphi environment. This shows the Delphi *Default* layout.

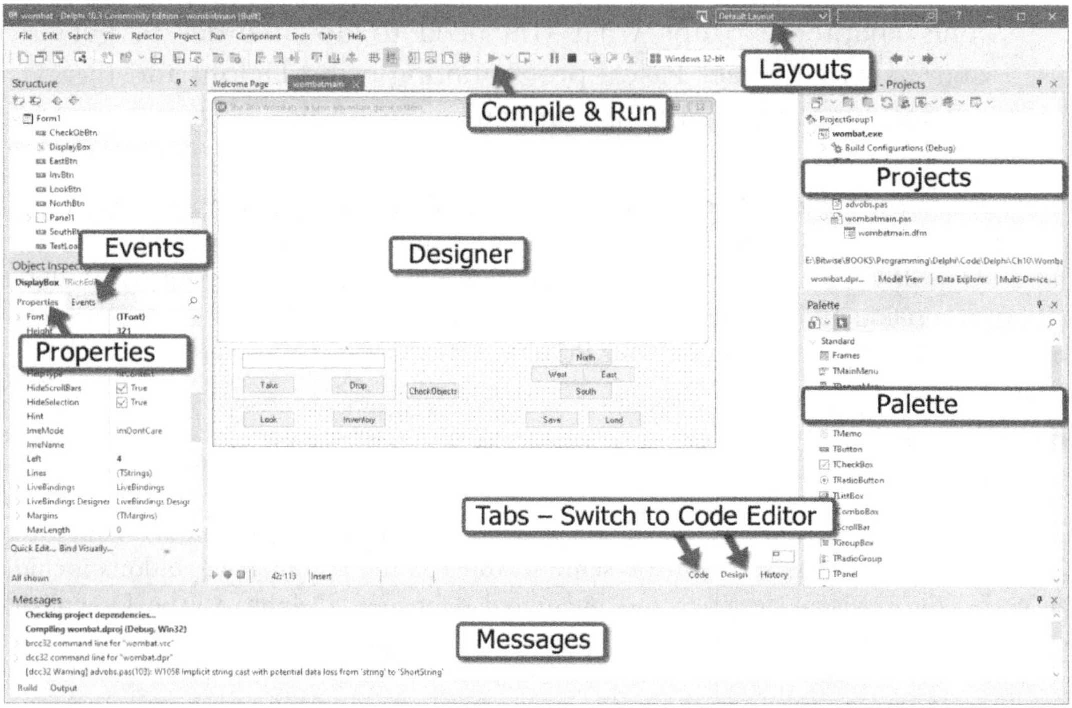

Layouts	Here you can select predefined layouts which change the appearance and positions of windows.
Compile & Run	Click the Green arrow-head symbol to compile your project and run it (or make a selection from the *Run* menu).
Projects	The Projects window lists one or more Delphi projects and all the code files of each project.
Palette	The Palette provides access to groups of components which can be dragged and dropped onto the form.
Designer	The Designer is where you can design a user interface by dragging components onto a form.
Tabs: Code/Design	Click the *Code* and *Design* tabs under the editor to switch from form design to code editing.

Events	Click the *Events* tab to create and edit the code of 'event-handling' functions for the selected component.
Properties	Click the *Properties* tab to display and edit visual properties of the selected component.
Messages	*Errors* (serious), *warnings* (less serious) and other messages relating to the code in your project are shown here.

Your First Program

In order to begin programming in Delphi, you need to select a project type. Various different project types are available. In this book, we will be generally the Windows VCL Application project type. VCL stands for 'Visual Component Library' and this project type supports drag-and-drop design using the components shown in Delphi's Palette window. If you are a Visual Studio programmer, you might think of the VCL as the approximate Delphi equivalent of Windows Forms.

Create a New Project

Follow these steps to start work on a new project…

- Start Delphi
- Select *File, New, Windows VCL Application – Delphi*

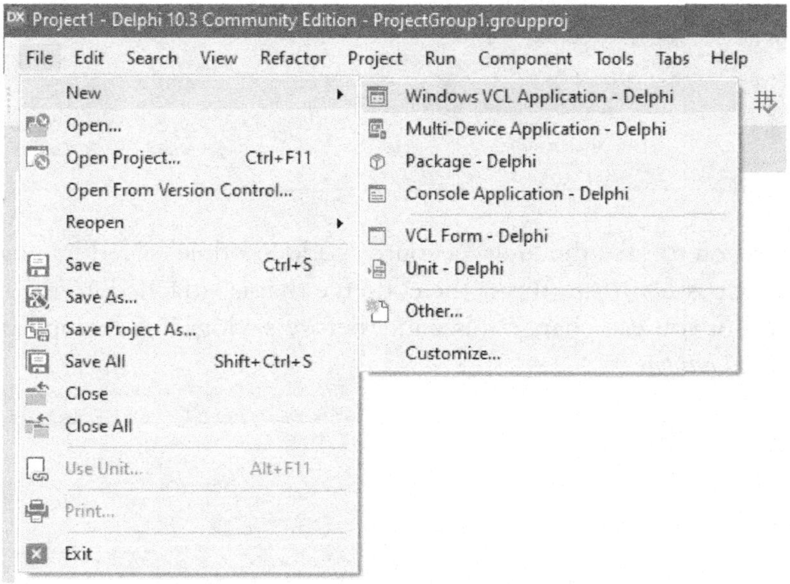

Delphi will create a new VCL project and load a blank form which is where you will design the user interface for your program. You should now name your project and save it to disk.

Save the Project

- Select *File, Save*
- In the *Save Project As* dialog, browse to a subdirectory
- Enter a name (with the *.dproj* extension) in the *File name* field
- Click *Save*

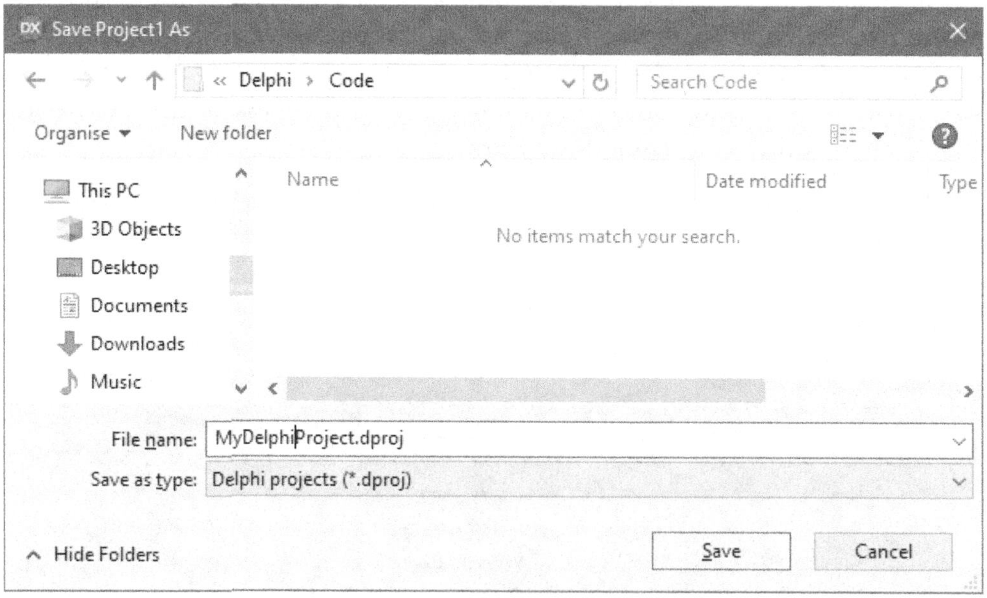

Delphi will prompt you to save the 'unit' (a source code 'module' saved in a named file). The default unit name is *Unit1.pas* (this is the code file that is 'attached' to the main form of the application) but you can change this name before saving. For example, you might decide to call it *MainUnit.pas*.

Delphi Projects

When you create a project it will be shown in Delphi's *Projects* window. You may load a 'Project Group' which contains more than one project. Here, for example, I have three projects named *Project1*, *bookobs2* and *wombat*. The code (*.pas*) files and visual forms (*.dfm*) files are shown on branches beneath the project name. Double-click a file to load it into the editor. You can double-click a project name in order to activate it (so it is the project that will be compiled and run). The name of the active project is shown in bold.

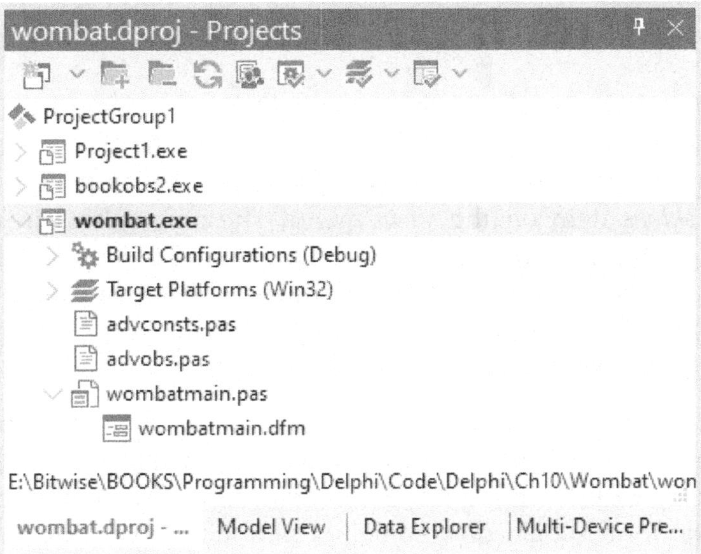

Project Files

Confusingly, Delphi projects may be loaded from files with either the *.dpr* or the *.dproj* extension. If you save a single project, it will create both a *.dpr* and a *.dproj* file. The *.dpr* file contains Pascal code to start your program. The *.dproj* file contains XML format configuration information. If you load several projects into a project group and then save that group (right-click the top node in the *Projects* window and select *Save Project Group As*) a *.groupproj* file is created. If you are used to Visual Studio, you may think of the Project Group as being like a Visual Studio Solution.

Design the Interface

If you followed the steps given to create and save a new project, you will now be ready to design and code an application. Make sure the Palette is visible. Normally the Palette is shown at the right of the screen. If you can't see it, click the *View* menu then *Tool Windows* and *Palette*. The Palette contains numerous ready-to-use components such as `TButton` and `TCheckBox`. The components are arranged in groups. You may need to click a heading (such as *Standard*) to expand the group and show the controls.

Delphi Desktop Layouts

The windows and toolbars of the Delphi environment may look different than shown in my screenshots if you select an alternative Desktop Layout. These can be activated from the *Desktops* item on the *View* menu. The screenshots in this book show the *Default* view. The *Classic Undocked* view switches to the layout that was standard in older versions of Delphi. In that layout the components are arranged in tabbed horizontal palettes at the top of the screen.

This is how to create a very simple visual interface. In the Palette, make sure the *Standard* section is expanded (click the heading to expand it). Click `TButton`. Hold down the left mouse button to drag it onto the blank form. Release the mouse button to drop a button onto the form. The form should now contain a button labelled 'Button1' which is the button object's name.

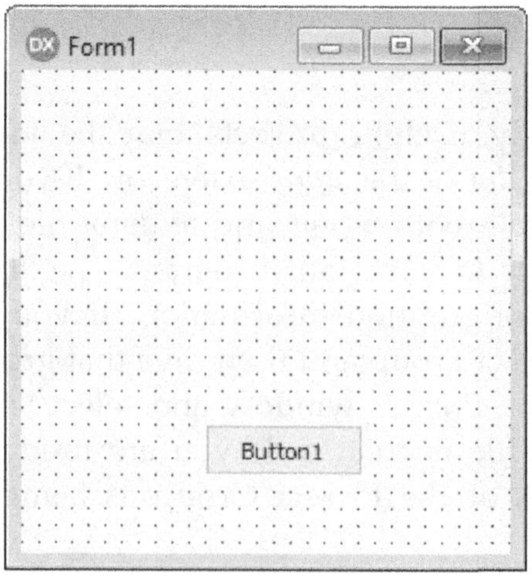

In a similar way, drag and drop a `TEdit` from the Toolbox onto the form. This will be given the name '*Edit1*'.

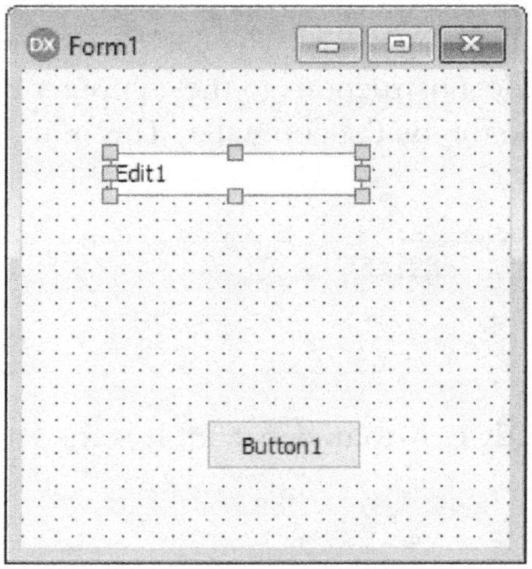

In order to make something happen when the button is clicked, we need to handle the mouse-click 'event'. Delphi makes it easy to do that. Double-click `Button1` on the form. That will automatically create a named bit of code or 'procedure' like this:

```
procedure TForm1.Button1Click(Sender: TObject);
begin
end;
```

All you have to do now is write some Pascal code between the `begin` and `end` of that procedure. I want to make the text of the `Edit1` component display `'Hello world'`. To do that, you can edit the procedure so that it contains the code shown below – be careful to include all the special characters and punctuation such as `:=` and ; exactly as shown:

```
TForm1.Button1Click(Sender: TObject);
begin
    Edit1.Text := 'Hello world';
end;
```

Now press the `F9` function key to run the program and click the button to verify that `'Hello world'` pops up in the Edit box.

A First Delphi Program

Object Pascal is a 'high level' language. It lets you write programs using human-readable instructions and pieces of data such as numbers. The Delphi compiler translates the Object Pascal code into 'machine code' (instructions to the computer hardware) to create an 'executable' program which can be run by the computer. This is an example of a piece of Object Pascal code:

AgeTest

```
if (age > 12) and (age < 20) then
    teenager := true;
```

While this isn't quite English, it is fairly easy to understand. It is the Pascal shorthand for this English sentence:

If your age is greater than 12 and less than 20 then you are a teenager.

This piece of code forms part of a sample program provided (in the source code archive which you should have downloaded by now, see page 7) for this chapter. The code for each chapter is placed into its own subdirectory. The *AgeTest.dproj* program is located in the *Ch1\AgeTest* subdirectory.

The *AgeTest* program has a user interface which includes a button, a scrollbar and four labels. The only label of any real interest is the one centered beneath the scrollbar which has the name *AgeLabel*. This is what the program looks like when you run it:

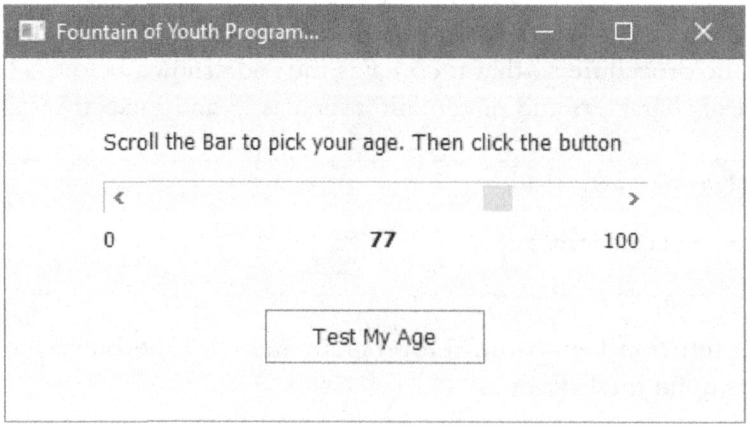

When the user moves the tab along the scrollbar the number shown in *AgeLabel* is updated to show its position between 0 and 100. When the button is clicked, the test shown on the previous page examines the value of the variable `age`, which is an integer that represents the value of the scroll bar's position.

If the value of the age variable falls between 13 and 19, the message `'You are a teenager.'` is shown. A different message is displayed for any other age. This is the code for this program (note that some the code found in the archive also includes some explanatory comments which are omitted from this listing):

AgeTest

```
procedure TForm1.Button1Click(Sender: TObject);
var
    age : integer;
    teenager : Boolean;
begin
    age := ScrollBar1.Position;
    teenager := false;
    if (age > 12) and (age < 20) then
        teenager := true;
    if teenager then
        ShowMessage('You are a teenager.')
    else
        ShowMessage('You are no teenager!');
end;
```

If you look at the code supplied in the archive, you'll see that the file *Age1.pas* contains considerably more code than is shown in the listing above. This code includes the unit name `Age1`, then the keyword `interface` followed by a definition of the Form:

```
unit Age1;

interface

uses
    SysUtils, WinTypes, WinProcs, Messages, Classes, Graphics, Controls,
    Forms, Dialogs, StdCtrls;

type
    TForm1 = class(TForm)
// ... and some more code
```

For now, you don't need to be concerned with any of that code, which was all automatically written by Delphi. The Appendix (*Anatomy of a Delphi Unit*) gives an explanation of this code if you are interested.

To try out this program, load and run the *AgeTest.dproj* project (press F9 or select *Run* from the *Run* menu). Move the scroll bar to pick an age and then click the button. Try various different ages to check that the message correctly determines which ages define 'teenager'. If you are completely new to Pascal programming, don't worry if you can't make sense of all the code in this program. That will all be explained in later chapters.

What is Object Pascal?

Before we start doing some serious programming, let me say a few words about the Object Pascal language that we will use throughout this book. Object Pascal is an object oriented version of the Pascal language. We'll be doing Object Oriented Programming (OOP) from the outset but I won't explain OOP in depth until Chapter 7. There are, in fact, several versions of Object Pascal but we are only concerned with the version supported by Delphi.

The original version of Pascal (which was not object oriented) was created in the late 1960s by the Swiss computer scientist Niklaus Wirth and named after the 17th Century French mathematician and philosopher Blaise Pascal.

Pascal was designed to be clear and well-structured. It was intended to be used "to teach programming as a systematic discipline based on certain fundamental concepts clearly and naturally reflected by the language"[1].

Over the years there have been many different versions of Pascal. One of the most famous was the Turbo Pascal compiler designed by the software company Borland in the early 1980s. Other Pascal-like languages, developed by Wirth, include Modula-2 and Oberon. Delphi is the most successful, and widely used, present-day implementation of Pascal.

---

[1] "Pascal User Manual and Report" 2nd Edition, 1975, p. 133, Wirth, N.

Chapter 2 – Fundamentals of Pascal

If you've never programmed before or if you've programmed but not in Pascal, this chapter will explain how to get started.

At first sight, even a short piece of program code may look both daunting and illogical. Take this code fragment, for example:

```
i := 1;
i := i + 1;
```

If a programmer were to read this out aloud, he or she you would probably say "*i equals 1. i equals i plus 1*". Taken literally, this doesn't make sense. In the example above, the first line of code clearly states that something called `i` equals 1. But it then appears to contradict itself by saying that that this same `i` equals itself *plus* 1 – in other words, 2.

Variables

In the code `i := 1;` the name or 'identifier' `i` is a variable. Variables are identifiers to which values may be assigned. They are called variables because their values may vary when new values are assigned to them.

Assignment

Common sense tells us that something always equals itself. An orange can't suddenly become two oranges. So how can an `i` suddenly become `i + 1`? The answer is that it can't. The *colon-equals-sign* `:=` in the code above does not test for equality. It assigns a value. The correct English translation of the two code lines above would be:

Code	**Translation**
`i := 1;`	*"Assign 1 to i"*
`i := i + 1;`	*"Add 1 to the value of i. Then assign the new value to i."*

To get a better understanding of how this works, load and load and run the *vars.dproj* project (from the *\Ch2* directory of the code archive) in Delphi. Click the first button a few times. When you click the button, this line of code executes:

vars

```
i := i + 1;
```

:= The Assignment Operator

The `:=` operator assigns the value on its right to the variable on its left. Look at this:

```
i := i + 1;
```

Here, the value which is calculated by `i + 1` is assigned to the variable on the left, which here is the variable `i`. So if `i` initially had the value 5, the expression `i + 1` would calculate the value 6, that value would then be assigned to `i`. So `i` now has the value 6.

The result of adding 1 to `i` is shown in the label to the right of the first button. Every time you click the button, the value of `i` goes up (that is, it is 'incremented') by 1. In this program, `i` begins with the value 0 so after five clicks it has the value 5:

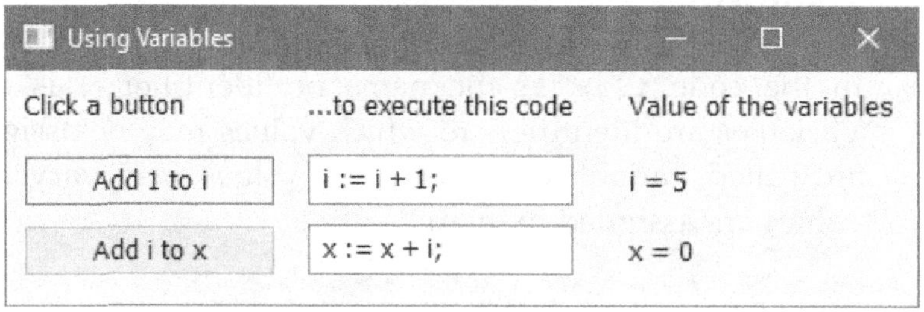

Now try clicking the second button a few times. This sets the value of a second variable, `x`, by adding the value of `i` to the current value of `x`. For example, if the value of `i` is 5 and the value of `x` is 0, when you click the second button, the value of `x` will become 5:

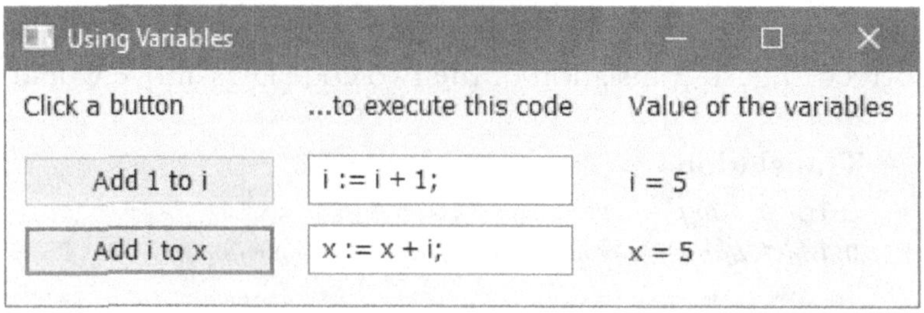

Click the first button two more times to set `i` to 7. Now if you click the second button again, the current value of `i` (7) is added to the current value of `x` (5). You end up with `x` being assigned the new value, 12:

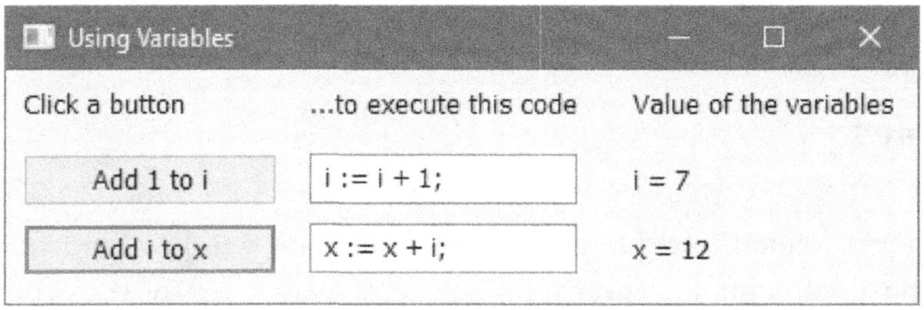

Using Variables

If it is still running, shut down the *vars* project by clicking its 'close' (X) button or pressing the **ALT-F4** keys. Now, let's take a look at the code itself. In the Delphi design view, double-click the second button labelled '*Add i to x*' on the form. This will place your cursor inside the editor on the piece of code which executes when the button is clicked in the running application:

```
x := x + i;
```

Notice that the code in this file is divided up into separate blocks called *procedures*. Most of these procedures are created automatically by Delphi and you don't need to be concerned with them for now.

I have also written one procedure myself, which I have named `ShowValues`. You may need to scroll up the code to find this. You will see that its full name is `procedure TForm1.ShowValues`:

vars

```
procedure TForm1.ShowValues;
begin
    ILabel.Caption := 'i = ' + IntToStr(i);
    XLabel.Caption := 'x = ' + IntToStr(x);
end;
```

Here `TForm1` refers to the form itself so you can think of the `ShowValues` procedure as 'belonging' to the form. This will be explained more fully when we explore Object Orientation in Chapter 7. The `ShowValues` procedure contains code which displays the current values of the `x` and `i` variables in two labels on the form. A label's Caption is a string (a piece of text) and `IntToStr()` is a function that converts an integer value to a string. We shall be discussing procedures and functions in the next chapter. The really important thing to notice for the present is how the two variables, `i` and `x`, are created and used.

Declaring Variables

If you have the *vars* project loaded into Delphi, expand the code window, and find the section marked with the comment: `{ Declaration of variables }`. Any text enclosed between the curly bracket characters is a comment. Comments are there for explanatory purposes and are ignored by the compiler. Beneath this comment is the following code:

vars

```
var
   i : integer;
   x : integer;
```

This is where the two variables, `i` and `x`, are declared. In Pascal it is obligatory to declare variables before using them. Unlike in some other languages, variable declarations cannot be 'mixed in' with executable code. A Pascal variable declaration section always begins with the keyword `var`. Beneath this you can enter a list of one or more variables. Each variable must have a unique name followed by a valid data type. In the present case, both variables are whole numbers of the `integer` type.

There are also two bits of punctuation that are required when declaring variables. First, you must separate the variable name from its type with a colon '`:`' character. And you must terminate each declaration with a semicolon '`;`' character. Alternatively, you could create a list of variables of the same type, with the variable names separated by commas as follows:

```
var
    i, x : integer;
```

Having been declared towards the top of the code, these variables are ready for use in any of the procedures beneath them. However, consider what would happen if the first piece of code that used these variables was:

```
x := x + i;
```

Up to now the variables have been declared but no values have been assigned to them. You should be sure to assign a value to every variable prior to using it. In fact, if you don't assign values, Delphi may (in some cases) automatically assign 'default values'. You should not rely on this, however.

Always explicitly assign some meaningful value before using a variable. In the present case, you'll see that the following assignments have been made in the procedure named `TForm1.FormCreate`, which executes when the Form object is created when the application is first run:

```
i := 0;
x := 0;
```

Variables and Data Types

Earlier on, I said that *variables* are so called because their values can vary. We've seen, for example, how the values of an integer variable can be repeatedly changed by adding numbers to it. But while the value of a variable may change, its data *type* does not. Once you've declared `x` to be an integer, you can't suddenly decide you'd prefer it to be a string (that is, a piece of text). Once an integer, always an integer.

Fixed-Type Variables

In some languages, such as Ruby and Python, it *is* possible to change the data type of a variable. Many languages, such as C and Pascal are 'strongly-typed', so once a variable is declared to be of a specific type, that type cannot be changed. Object Pascal does, in fact, provide one type of variable called a `Variant` whose type can be changed. See the Appendix for more information. Variants will not be used in this book.

Variables are the building blocks of programming. So it's worth taking the time at the outset to understand precisely what they are and how they work. In essence, you can think of a variable a sort of a labelled container – a programming equivalent of a cardboard box.

Imagine that you have three boxes on your desk: one contains petty cash, a second contains cash for food and drink and a third contains your fuel money. Each of these boxes looks the same as the others, so to help you tell them apart you stick labels on them: *pettyCash*, *entertainmentsBudget* and *fuelMoney*.

Finally, you put 10 units of currency (integers) into each box. The boxes are your variables and the labels are the variable names. Each variable has been assigned a data-type (`integer`). I also want to keep track of the money in my wallet. To represent this in a program we would declare these four variables:

cash

```
var
    pettyCash,
    entertainmentsBudget,
    fuelMoney,
    wallet : integer;
```

I put 10 currency units into each box, so my program needs to assign 10 to each variable. Once again, I make these assignments in the `FormCreate` procedure which runs when the program starts:

```
pettyCash := 10;
entertainmentsBudget := 10;
fuelMoney := 10;
```

Currently my wallet is empty so I assign 0 to that variable:

```
wallet := 0;
```

To see how this works in a real application, load the *cash* sample application into Delphi.

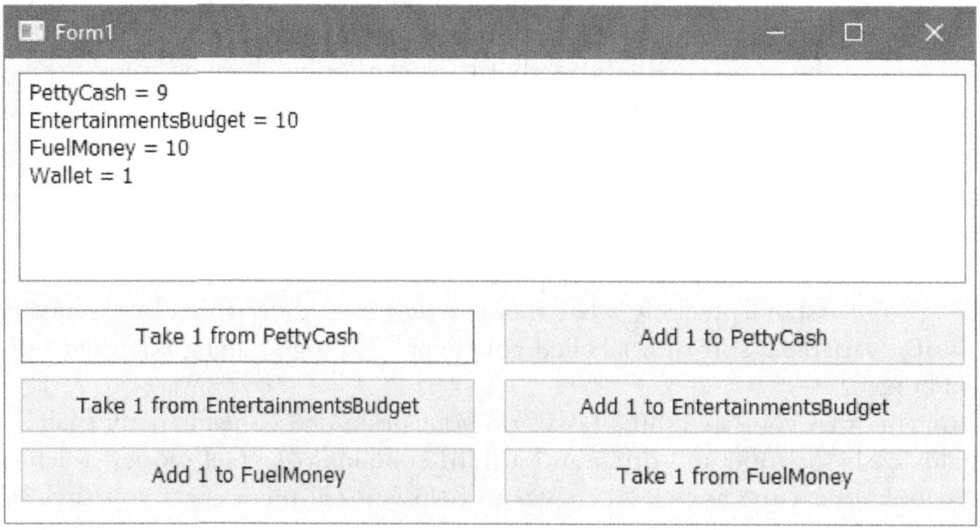

Run the application and click the first (top-left) button on the form to subtract 1 from the value of the `pettyCash` variable. When you do this, 1 is added to the value of the `wallet` variable. The Memo box at the top of the form displays the current values of each of the variables.

You can click other buttons to take 1 from your `wallet` and add it to one of the other cash boxes. Here is the code that executes when you click the button labelled *'Take 1 from PettyCash'*:

```
procedure TForm1.FromPCashBtnClick(Sender: TObject);
begin
    pettyCash := pettyCash - 1;
    wallet := wallet + 1;
    ShowValues;
end;
```

Here the procedure `FromPCashBtnClick` (which 'belongs' to `TForm1`) contains three lines of code. The first line subtracts 1 from the value of `pettyCash` and assigns the new value back to `pettyCash`. The second line similarly adds 1 to `wallet`. The third line calls another procedure called `ShowValues`. 'Calling' a procedure causes the code in that procedure to be run. `ShowValues` displays formatted output to show the variable values in the Memo.

Pascal is Case-Insensitive

Object Pascal is a case-*insensitive* language. That means that if you have a variable named `myVar`, you may refer to it using a different mix of uppercase and lowercase letters such as `MyVar` or `myVAR`. Many other programming languages are case-*sensitive* and do not permit this.

Notice that I've used quite long variable names in this program. This is because descriptive variable names make your programs easier to understand. Long variable names are no less 'efficient' than short variable names. The Pascal compiler converts your variables into machine code before the program is run and by that stage your variable names no longer exist.

So, be sure to give your variables descriptive names which make it clear what your code is intended to do. To illustrate this, let's look at an example of some code that uses very short variable names.

Code Fragment 1

```
if (a > 45) and (p = m) then b := 1000;
```

The single-letter variables here make it impossible to understand what this code is trying to do. Now look at this piece of code:

Code Fragment 2

```
if (age   > 45) and (position = manager) then
    bonus := 1000;
```

You'll probably agree that the second piece of code is much easier to understand than the first piece of code. But, as far as the computer is concerned, the two pieces of code have exactly the same meaning. Before the program runs, the Pascal compiler translates your original source code into 'machine code' which are instructions to the computer hardware. In the process of compilation, the names you've given to variables are discarded. So a variable called `b` will result in the same piece of machine code as a variable called `bonus`. It makes sense, therefore, to make a habit of using meaningful variable names. Long, descriptive names don't change the way your program runs but they do make them easier to understand.

Incidentally, notice how the value 1000 has been entered in the code. When you specify numerical values, make sure you don't use commas. If you do use commas, the compiler will tell you that you've made an error:

```
{This is wrong}
bonus := 1,000;

{This is correct}
bonus := 1000;
```

Naming Variables

In Delphi, variable names may contain alphanumeric characters – that is, both letters of the alphabet and numbers. You cannot use a number as the *first* character of a variable name, however. Variables cannot use the same names as pre-defined 'keywords' of the Pascal language such as `procedure`, `if` or `begin`. See the Appendix for more on *Naming Conventions*.

'if' Statements

Look back again at *Code Fragment 2*. You will see that this introduces an important new feature. Before an assignment is made to the `bonus` variable, a test has been done to check the values of the `age` and `position` variables. Tests of this sort provide a way for your programs to choose between two or more alternative actions. Often you may want to use just one test condition like this:

```
if (age  > 45) then
    bonus := 1000;
```

However, the test in *Code Fragment 2* uses two conditions, each of which is enclosed in 'round brackets' or parentheses. In Pascal the parentheses are optional but they are recommended in order to avoid potential ambiguities:

```
if (age  > 45) and (position = manager) then
    bonus := 1000;
```

Operators and Tests

The first condition, `(age > 45)`, uses the `>` symbol which is Pascal's *'greater than'* operator. The second test, `(position = manager)`, uses `=` which is Pascal's *equality* operator.

The two conditions have been linked using the `and` keyword. This means that both conditions must be true in order for the next statement, `bonus := 1000`, to run. If either condition fails then that statement will be bypassed. The program will go on to run the next bit of code after the bypassed statement.

Assignment and Equality Operators

It is easy to confuse the assignment operator, *colon-equals* (`:=`) with the equality operator, *equals* (`=`).

`:=` is used to give a value to a variable.

`=` is used to test the value of a variable.

'if...else' Statements

Often, you may want to provide an alternative action if a test fails. For example, you might want to give a different bonus if the employee is *not* a manager over the age of 45. You can do this easily by adding on an `else` clause after the `if` like this:

```
if (age  > 45) and (position = manager) then
    bonus := 1000
else
    bonus := 200;
```

The words `if`, `then` and `else` are Pascal *keywords*. That means they are an essential part of the Pascal language.

The basic syntax of an *if..then..else* statement can be summarised as follows:

```
if <Some Condition> then
    <Do This>
else
    <Do This>
```

The items shown between angle brackets here are not real code. They indicate the kind of code which needs to be added at these positions. To see a working example, load up the *agetest* project (which we saw first in Chapter 1 and is found in the *Ch1* folder of the source code archive) and look at the file, *age1.pas*, in the editor.

Boolean Values

In this code, the `age` variable is an teenager variable is an `integer` and the `teenager` variable is a `Boolean`:

```
var
    age : integer;
    teenager : Boolean;
```

`Boolean` is a data type that can have just one of two values, `true` or `false`. In the *agetest* program, the code starts by setting the `teenager` variable to `false`. It is only assigned a `true` value if the `age` variable has a value that is greater than 12 (`age > 12`) and less than 20 (`age < 20`).

agetest

```
teenager := false;
if (age > 12) and (age < 20) then
    teenager := true;
if teenager then
    ShowMessage('You are a teenager.')
else
    ShowMessage('You are no teenager!');
```

Let's take a close look at this code. The first test has no surprises. It uses a simple `if...then` test with no `else` clause. If both conditions `(age > 12)` and also `(age < 20)` are found to be true then the next line executes and the `teenager` variable is set to `true`. Otherwise `teenager` retains the `false` value which was assigned to it at the outset. Now we come to another test. This one forms the first part of an `if...then...else` statement.

This starts by testing if the `teenager` variable is `true`:

```
if teenager
```

Note that this is a 'shorthand' way of testing the value of a `Boolean` variable. It could be rewritten in a longer form like this:

```
if (teenager = true)
```

When a `Boolean` variable has the value `true`, an `if` test will succeed. When it has the value `false`, an `if` test will fail. If the `teenager` variable has been assigned a `true` value then the test condition evaluates to `true` and the next line of code runs:

```
ShowMessage('You are a teenager.')
```

If the condition evaluates to `false` then the code following the `else` keyword runs instead:

```
ShowMessage('You are no teenager!');
```

In this code, `ShowMessage` is the name of a procedure provided for us by Delphi. When the procedure executes, it pops up a dialog box containing the string that we pass to it. In Pascal, strings must be enclosed between single-quotation marks. Notice too that, as with the variable declarations, each code line is terminated with a semicolon. The semicolon is Pascal's 'statement separator'. You must put a semicolon at the end of every complete statement. An exception to the rule occurs prior to the `else` keyword. In Pascal you must not use a semicolon at the end of the line preceding an `else` clause.

Now Get Coding!

The best way to consolidate your knowledge of the topics described in this book is by doing lots of hands-on coding. Try to make a habit of modifying the code in the sample programs provided. For example, try adapting the *cash* program so that it does not allow any of the three variables to have negative values. To do this you will need to test if the values become less than zero. You will need an `if` test to verify this. You might even try adding an `else` clause to pop up a message using the `ShowMessage` procedure to warn users that they are about to go into debt!

Constants

Sometimes you may want to ensure than an item's value cannot be changed. For example, in a financial program, you might have a fixed tax rate; in mathematics, you wouldn't want the value of π to be changed. When you want to ensure that a value remains unaltered, you should declare it to be a constant using the keyword, `const`, like this:

consts

```
// These are constants - their values cannot be changed
const
    myConstStr = 'Hello world';
    myConstInt = 10;
    myConstDbl = 2.5;
```

The values of constants cannot be changed so this is *not* permitted:

```
myConstStr := 'Goodbye Mars';
myConstInt := 25;
myConstDbl := 5.6;
```

Note that you do not need to specify the *type* of a constant. In fact, if you do so, you may be able to change the value in your code! Typed constants are explained in the Appendix.

Constant Naming

In the *consts* sample program, I gave my constants names in mixed upper and lowercase letters like this: `myConstStr`. In fact, it is common practice to write constant names all in uppercase, sometimes with underscores separating the 'words' like this: `MY_CONST_STR`.

Remember, however, that since Pascal is case-*insensitive* even if you declare your constants in uppercase, they can be written in lowercase or mixed case and they will still be valid (unlike in case-sensitive language such as C or Java), so it would *not* be an error to could refer to the constant named `MY_CONST_STR` as `My_Const_Str`.

Elements of a Pascal Program

I've already mentioned quite a few things that go to make up a computer program written in Pascal. In later chapters, I'll look at many more things such as functions, procedures, classes and objects. For now, though, here is a summary of some of the most important program elements that we have covered so far.

Keywords

A keyword is an identifier that is reserved for use by the programming language. For example, in Pascal, `begin` and `end`, which are used to delimit blocks of code, are keywords.

Types

A 'type' describes a particular type of data. For example, a whole number may be declared to be an `integer`. A sequence of characters may be declared to be a `string`. This is an example of two variables of the `integer` and `string` types:

```
var
    myInt : integer;
    myString : string;
```

In Pascal, once a variable has been declared to be of a specific type it can only be assigned data of that type, like this:

```
myInt := 10;
myString := 'Hello ';
```

It is an error to assign data of the wrong type:

```
myInt := 'Hello ';    // This is an error!
myString := 10;       // This is an error!
```

An exception to this rule is the `variant` type which is described in the Appendix.

Variables

A variable is an identifier that is defined by the programmer to hold some special type of value. In Pascal a variable is declared after the `var` keyword. It must be followed by a colon, the *type* of the variable and a semicolon. Different values (of the appropriate type) may be assigned to the variable during the execution of a program.

Constants

In Pascal a constant is declared after the `const` keyword. It must be followed by an equals sign, a value, and a semicolon. The value of a constant (with the exception of 'typed constants', explained in the Appendix) cannot be changed during the execution of the program and no new values may be assigned to it.

Operators

An operator is a special character or combination of characters that indicates that some sort of operation will be done on one or more data items. Common operators are the arithmetic operators such as `+`, `-`, `*` and `/` and the assignment operator `:=` which assigns a value on its right to a variable on its left.

Comments

It is a good idea to add comments to your programs to describe what each section is supposed to do. Pascal lets you insert comments between curly brackets `{ }`:

```
{ This is a Pascal comment }
```

Alternatively, you can put comments inside round brackets enclosing asterisks `(* *)`:

```
(* This is also a Pascal comment *)
```

You should standardize on one type of comment (personally I prefer curly brackets) as a general rule. Then, if you want to comment out a block of code that already contain comments, you can do so by enclosing it in the alternative style of comment delimiters. Here, for example, the `(*` and `*)` delimiters comment out (and therefore make invisible to the Delphi compiler) both the code and the comment in curly brackets:

```
(*
  begin
     x := y; { I wonder what this means? }
  end;
*)
```

In addition to these block-delimiting comments, Object Pascal also lets you use 'line comments' that begin with two slash characters `//` and extend to the end of the current line. Line comments may either comment out an entire line or any part of a line which may include code before the `//` characters. These are examples of line comments:

```
// This is a full-line comment
    if Teenager then // this comment follows some code
```

Chapter 3 – Procedures and Functions

Pascal makes a distinction between a function which returns a value and a procedure which does not. This chapter explains functions and procedures.

Up to now the biggest program we've written has been only about a dozen lines in length. Programs of any complexity are likely to contain many hundreds or thousands of lines of code. Commercial applications such as word processors and databases may contain millions of lines of code. In order to make long programs understandable and maintainable they are divided up into named blocks of code which, in Pascal, are called functions and procedures.

Procedures

A procedure is a named block of code which does not return a value. A procedure starts with the keyword `procedure` followed by a name (of your choice) and a semicolon. The code inside the procedure must be delimited by the keywords, `begin` and `end`.

Let's look at a simple example. In the *proc* project I have created a form containing one Edit field and two buttons. I want the user to enter his or her name in the Edit box. When one of the buttons is clicked, a message box pops up and shows a personalized greeting. Run the application and try it out. Notice that if you leave the Edit box blank, an error message pops up.

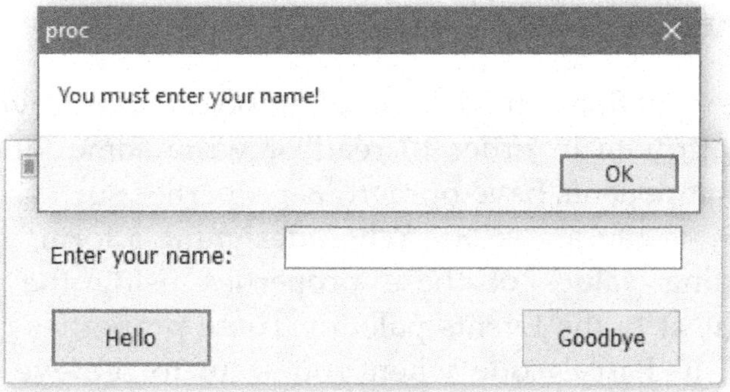

Delphi automatically creates procedures to handle 'events' such as mouse clicks. You can auto-create these event-handlers either by double-clicking a component on a form to create its default event-handler (for a button, that will create a mouse-click event-handler) or you can double-click the blank area to the right of a specific event name (such as `OnKeyDown` which responds to a keyboard key being held down) in the Events palette in order to create an event-handler for that event.

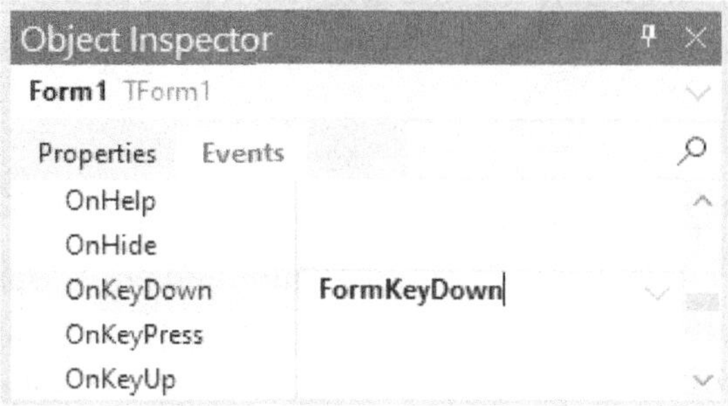

You will see that each of the two buttons on the form in the *proc* project contains code that performs an `if` test to determine whether the `Edit1` field is empty, that is if its `Text` property equals an empty string (`''`). Here is the code inside the `TForm1.HelloBtnClick` procedure:

proc

```
procedure TForm1.HelloBtnClick(Sender: TObject);
begin
    if Edit1.Text = '' then
       ShowErrorMsg
    else
       ShowMessage('Hello ' + Edit1.Text);
    Caption := 'This is the last line in HelloBtnClick';
end;
```

Properties

A property defines an attribute of an object and provides access to that attribute in order to read or write some kind of data. Visual components have numerous properties such as a Button's `Text`, `Font`, `Height` and `Width`. When designing a form, you can set the starting values of these properties using the Properties palette (next to the Events palette). These properties can also be accessed in Pascal code when you want to retrieve or change their values.

Procedure Calls

In the code of `TForm1.HelloBtnClick`, if the `Edit1` field is empty (that is, if the `Text` property of `Edit1` is an empty string: `''`), the code immediately following the `if` test runs. This contains the name of the procedure `ShowErrorMsg`. This is a 'procedure call'. When the running program encounters the `ShowErrorMsg` procedure call, it jumps straight to that procedure:

```
procedure ShowErrorMsg;
begin
    ShowMessage('You must enter your name!');
end;
```

The program now runs the code in the `ShowErrorMsg` procedure. Once it has done that, the program returns to the code immediately after the procedure call. In the present case, this means that the line following `else` in the `HelloBtnClick` procedure will be skipped (since that only executes when the `if` test is false) and the final line, which places text into the Form's `Caption`, will be executed:

```
Caption := 'This is the last line in HelloBtnClick';
```

You can follow this flow of execution yourself. Run the application again. Notice that, initially the form's caption reads *'You haven't clicked a button yet'*.

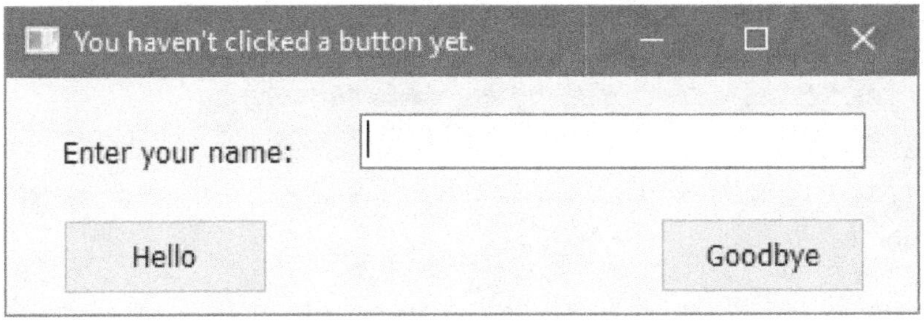

Leave the Edit field blank and click the button labelled *'Hello'*. Since `Edit1.Text` is blank, the first line of code after the `if` test will be run. This calls `ShowErrMsg`:

```
if Edit1.Text = '' then
    ShowErrorMsg
```

The program now runs the code in the `ShowErrMsg` procedure which pops up an error message stating *'You must enter your name!'*. Notice that, as long as this message dialog is on screen, the Form's caption remains unchanged. It still says *'You haven't clicked a button yet'*. This is because the flow of this program's execution is stuck inside the `ShowErrorMsg` procedure until the dialog box is shut down.

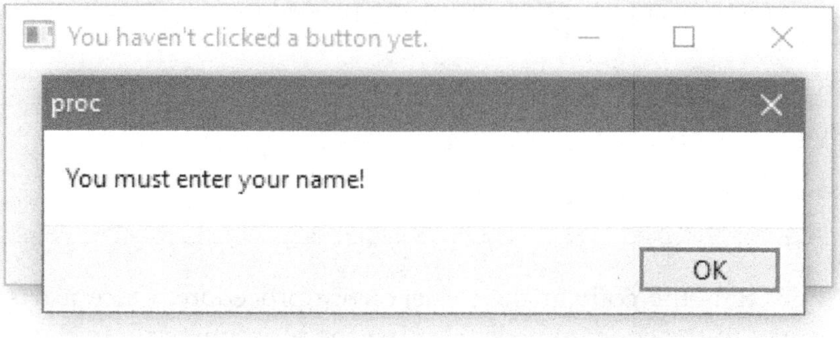

Close the message dialog by clicking its *OK* button. As soon as the dialog is closed, the flow of execution returns to the `HelloBtnClick` procedure and it runs the final line, which immediately changes the Form's caption to *'This is the last line in HelloBtnClick'*.

```
procedure TForm1.HelloBtnClick(Sender: TObject);
begin
  if Edit1.Text = '' then
    ShowErrorMsg
  else
    ShowMessage( 'Hello ' + Edit1.Text );
  Caption := 'This is the last line in HelloBtnClick';
end;
```

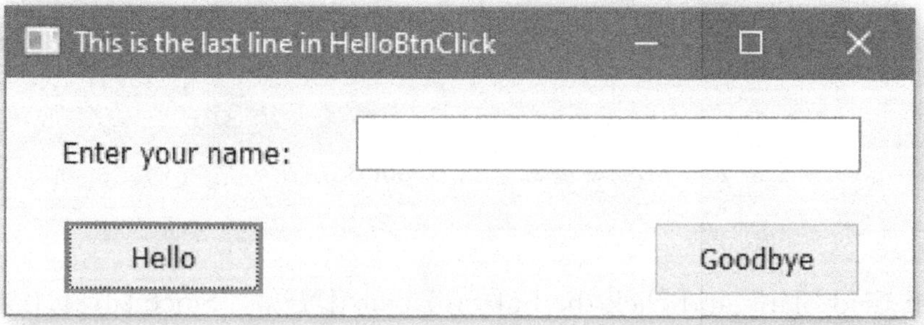

One of the great things about procedures is that they can be used time after time, whenever your program needs them. This avoids having to write the same code more than once. In the present case, for example, the `GoodbyeBtnClick` procedure also calls `ShowErrorMsg`:

```
procedure TForm1.GoodbyeBtnClick(Sender: TObject);
begin
    if Edit1.Text = '' then
       ShowErrorMsg
    else
       ShowMessage('Goodbye ' + Edit1.Text);
    Caption := 'This is the last line in GoodbyeBtnClick';
end;
```

In this simple program, the benefits of placing code inside procedures may not be all that obvious. Bear in mind, though, that in a real-life application, a procedure such as `ShowErrorMsg` could contain dozens of lines of code. And it might be used many times, throughout the program. By putting that code into a named procedure (which can be called whenever it is needed) you avoid having to rewrite the same lines of code time after time after time.

Bearing this principle in mind, if you look again at the *procs* program you may notice that it does, in fact, contain some lines of code that are repeated unnecessarily. The two *ButtonClick* procedures, `HelloBtnClick` and `GoodbyeBtnClick`, are almost identical. If I were decide to add some more buttons I would end up rewriting the same `if...else` test many times. Let's see if I can improve upon this by rewriting my code to avoid repetition.

Functions

Load up the *procfunc* project. If you run this, you'll see that it has similar behaviour to the previous program. When you've finished, close the application. In the form-designer, double-click the *'Hello'* button in order to locate the procedure `TForm1.HelloBtnClick` in the code editor:

procfunc

```
procedure TForm1.HelloBtnClick(Sender: TObject);
var
    msg: string;
begin
    msg := MsgFunc('Hello ', Edit1.Text);
    ShowMessage(msg);
end;
```

As you can see, there is much less code in this rewritten procedure. The `if...else` test from the previous version has vanished. In its place, there is a call to `MsgFunc`. Scroll up the code and find the following:

procfunc

```
function MsgFunc(greeting, username : string) : string;
begin
    if username = '' then
       MsgFunc := 'You must enter your name!'
    else
       MsgFunc := greeting + username;
end;
```

While this looks similar to a procedure, you will see that it is begins with the keyword `function` instead of the keyword `procedure`. A function is, essentially, just a procedure that *returns a value*. In Pascal, the type of the return value must be specified, following a colon, at the end of the function header. The `MsgFunc` function returns a string.

Parameters

Here `greeting` and `username` are special types of variables called 'parameters'. They represent two data items (or 'arguments') that have been passed to the `MsgFunc` function by the code that calls it. Here, both the `greeting` and `username` parameters are of the `string` data type. Once again, the data type is specified after a colon:

```
greeting, username : string
```

Inside the function body, these two parameters can be used just like ordinary variables. However, the parameter names are not 'visible' to code outside the function itself so they cannot be used elsewhere in your code. Parameters are explained in more detail later in this chapter.

The `if...else` test has been moved into the `MsgFunc` function. The code tests whether the parameter called `username` is an empty string. If it is an empty string, then the string `'You must enter your name!'` is assigned to `MsgFunc`, if is not an empty string, then the string formed by concatenating the two string parameters `greeting + username` is assigned to `MsgFunc`.

But what does it mean when you assign a value to the name of the function itself? In Pascal, this is one way of specifying the value that is returned from the function. According to its definition (the function 'header'), the `MsgFunc` function returns a string – because `string` is the data type following the colon:

```
function MsgFunc(greeting, username : string) : string;
```

Assigning a string to the function name, causes the function to return the assigned string. This assignment causes the `MsgFunc` function to return `'You must enter your name!'`:

```
MsgFunc := 'You must enter your name!'
```

Procedure and Function Syntax Summary

Let me quickly summarise how procedures and functions are used in Pascal. Note that in the code fragments shown below, the items shown between angle brackets `< >` are not 'real' code. In a working program, they would need to be replaced either by an actual data-type or by one or more identifier names as indicated (these must adhere to the same naming rules that apply to variables, as explained in Chapter 1 and summarised in the Appendix). The items shown between curly brackets `{ }` are optional:

```
function <FunctionName> {(<One or more parameters>) } : <ReturnType>;
begin
    {One or more lines of code}
    <FunctionName> := <SomeValue>;
end;

procedure <ProcedureName> {(<One or more parameters>)};
begin
    {One or more lines of code}
end;
```

Function Return Values

To specify the return value of a function using traditional Pascal syntax, you assign a value of the appropriate data type to the function name. Delphi provides an alternative way of specifying return values from functions. The return value can be specified using the word `result`, like this:

```
result := greeting + username;
```

In the *procfunc* project I've included an alternative version of the `MsgFunc` function (in a comment block) which uses `result` in order to return a value.

Passing Arguments

Now let's see how arguments are passed to a function or procedure. Look at the `MsgFunc` function in the *procfunc* project. Two string parameters `greeting` and `username` are listed between parentheses:

```
function MsgFunc(greeting, username : string) : string;
```

These parameters indicate that the function is expecting to receive some values from the code that called it. The number of values that are sent to the function must match the number of parameters in the function header. They must also match the parameter data type. This means that any code that calls the `MsgFunc` function must pass two strings to that function.

Look at `TForm1.HelloBtnClick`. You'll see that this code does, indeed, pass two strings to the `MsgFunc` function, the string `'Hello'` and the string contents (that is the `Text` property) of the `Edit1` component:

```
msg := MsgFunc('Hello ', Edit1.Text);
```

Just like a procedure-call, this function-call causes the running program to jump into the named function and run the code inside that function. Any values (arguments) sent to a procedure or function are assigned to the parameters occupying the same positions in the function header. In this case, the `greeting` and `username` parameters declared in the header of `MsgFunc` will be assigned the string `'Hello'` and the contents of `Edit1.Text`.

When this function has finished running, it returns a string value. The code in `TForm1.HelloBtnClick`, shown above assigns that value to a string variable, `msg`. If `Edit1.Text` is blank, then the second argument, whose value is assigned to the `username` parameter in the `MsgFunc` function, is an empty string (`''`) and so the `if...else` test returns the string shown here:

```
if username = '' then
    MsgFunc := 'You must enter your name!'
```

On the other hand, if `Edit1.Text` contains a string, such as `'Fred'`, then the `username` parameter will have the value `'Fred'`, so the code line after `else` runs and returns a concatenation of the two arguments, `'Hello ' + 'Fred'`:

```
MsgFunc := greeting + username;
```

Although it is normal to assign the return value to a variable of the same data type such as `msg` in the example above, this is not absolutely necessary. If you look at the code of `TForm1.GoodbyeBtnClick`, you'll see that the function-call to `MsgFunc` has been placed inside the parentheses following the call to `ShowMessage`:

```
ShowMessage(MsgFunc('Goodbye ', Edit1.Text));
```

This has the effect of executing the `MsgFunc` function and passing its *return value* as an argument to the `ShowMessage` procedure. `ShowMessage` is one of Delphi's pre-defined procedures and it can be used in exactly the same way as procedures you write yourself.

Procedures, Functions Or Methods?

In Object Oriented languages, such as Object Pascal, Java, C# and Ruby, procedures and functions are often called '*methods*'. That is because they provide a method (a 'way') for an object to perform some type of operation. We'll look at Object Orientation in Chapter 7. For now, it's sufficient to know that the word 'method' may describe either a procedure or a function.

Parameter Syntax

There are a few rules to be observed when specifying parameters in a function or procedure header. Each parameter must be followed by its data type preceded by a colon. For example, this procedure takes a single integer parameter:

```
procedure TimesTenProc(anumber : integer);
```

It is also possible to declare a list of parameters of the same type, in which case, each item in the list is separated by a comma. This procedure takes three string parameters:

```
procedure SomeStringsProc(s1, s2, s3 : string);
```

When a parameter list includes parameters of different data types, each parameter or list of parameters is divided from any subsequent parameters by a semi-colon. This function takes one string, followed by two integer parameters. It returns a string:

```
function StrMultiply(msg : string; num1, num2 : integer) : string;
```

Arguments or Parameters?

To be formally correct, an '*argument*' describes the value that is sent to a procedure or method by the code that calls it. A '*parameter*' is the name declared in the procedure or function header. The parameters are initialized with the values of the arguments that are passed to a function or procedure. In fact, often programmers tend to use the terms *argument* and *parameter* interchangeably. The parameter names declared in a function header are commonly called the 'argument list'.

Var Parameters

Sometimes it may be useful for a function to 'return' more than one value to the code that called it. But a function can only explicitly return a single data item. So if you call a function (or procedure) with two integer variables, `num1` and `num2` and the function makes changes to the values of both variables, how would you pass the changed values back to the code that originally called the function? Remember that parameters names are like variables that are 'local' to a function and they cannot be accessed by code outside that function.

In fact, it turns out that it is possible for a procedure or function to change the values of parameters in such a way that those changes also affect the values of the variables that were passed as arguments. Load up the *varparam* project and find the `TForm1.Button1Click` procedure. This initializes six integer variables:

varparam

```
n1 := 1;
n2 := 2;
n3 := 3;
n4 := 4;
n5 := 5;
n6 := 6;
```

These six variables are passed as arguments to a procedure called `Meddle`:

```
Meddle(n1, n2, n3, n4, n5, n4 + n5);
```

The `Meddle` procedure adds 1 to each parameter:

```
procedure Meddle(var num1, num2, num3: integer;
                     num4, num5, num6: integer);
begin
    num1 := num1 + 1;
    num2 := num2 + 1;
    num3 := num3 + 1;
    num4 := num4 + 1;
    num5 := num5 + 1;
    num6 := num6 + 1;
end;
```

When the button is clicked, the *initial* variable values are displayed in the Memo:

```
Memo1.Lines.Add(Format('n1=%d, n2=%d, n3=%d, n4=%d, n5=%d, n6=%d',
[n1,n2,n3,n4,n5,n6]));
```

This is what is shown:

```
n1=1, n2=2, n3=3, n4=4, n5=5, n6=6
```

Then the variables are passed to the `Meddle` procedure. And the variable values are once again displayed in the Memo:

```
Meddle(n1, n2, n3, n4, n5, n6);
Memo1.Lines.Add(Format('n1=%d, n2=%d, n3=%d, n4=%d, n5=%d, n6=%d',
[n1,n2,n3,n4,n5,n6]));
```

Now this is what is shown:

```
n1=2, n2=3, n3=4, n4=4, n5=5, n6=6
```

The important thing to note is that, even though the `Meddle` procedure adds 1 to each of the six parameters, only the values of the first three variables (`n1`, `n2` and `n3`) have actually been altered back within the 'scope' of the procedure, `Button1Click`, from which `Meddle` was called.

Let's look at the Meddle procedure to see why this is the case:

```
procedure Meddle(var num1, num2, num3 : integer;
                     num4, num5, num6 : integer);
```

The first three integer parameters are preceded by the keyword var. This list of parameters is terminated by a semicolon. Then begins a list of three more parameters. These, however, are not preceded by the word var.

Incidentally, the fact that the second list of parameters is indented on a new line is irrelevant. In Pascal, indentation and line-breaks are used to improve readability. They have no effect on the meaning of the code.

The important thing to realize is that any parameter preceded by the word var is a *direct reference to the original variable* that was sent to the procedure. So the var parameter called num1 refers to precisely the same piece of data as the variable n1 in Button1Click. When 1 is added to num1 in the Meddle procedure, 1 is also added to n1 in Button1Click.

Parameters that are *not* preceded by the var keyword, on the other hand, are *copies* of the original data. So the num4 parameter, for instance, is assigned a new piece of data which has the same value as the argument passed at that position in the procedure-call which, in this case, is the variable n4. But the num4 parameter only exists inside the Meddle procedure. When the procedure finishes running, the num4 parameter is discarded. Any changes that were made to num4 inside Meddle are lost forever and have no effect on the code that called the procedure.

Format Strings

The Format function used in the code of the *varparam* project is useful for creating a string with values embedded into it:

```
Format('n1=%d, n2=%d, n3=%d, n4=%d, n5=%d, n6=%d',
[n1,n2,n3,n4,n5,n6])
```

Here, six integer variables, n1 to n6, are enclosed between square brackets and sent as the second argument to Format. The string passed as the first argument to Format includes six %d place-markers. The %d indicates that a decimal integer value is expected. Each of the six place-markers in sequence is replaced by the values of the six variables between square brackets. I'll have more to say about Format Strings in Chapter 5.

Value and Variable Parameters

The diagram below illustrates the difference between a `var` or 'variable' parameter which is passed a reference to the original variable; and a regular or 'value' parameter which is passed a new copy of the value of the original variable:

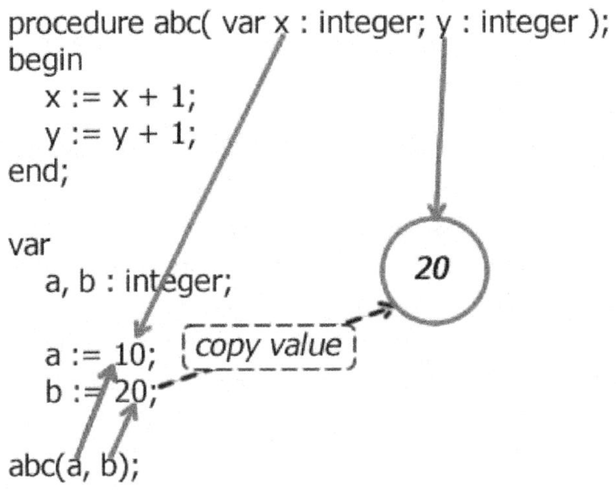

Here `x` is a `var` or 'variable' parameter and `y` is an ordinary or 'value' parameter. The procedure `abc()` is passed the `a` and `b` variables. The `var` parameter `x` refers to the same piece of data (10) as the variable `a`. But the `y` parameter is passed a *copy* of the value of `b`. So `b` refers to a different piece of data (stored at a different memory location) than `y`. As a consequence, any changes to `y` won't affect the value of `b`. But a change to `x` will change the value of `a` because both `a` and `x` refer to exactly the same piece of data.

If you find it hard to grasp the difference between variable and value parameters, try thinking of a 'real world' example. Let's imagine that the painting of the Mona Lisa is represented by a variable `mona_lisa` in a computer program.

If the Louvre Museum were to loan the *original* painting to an exhibition somewhere, that would be the equivalent of sending the variable `mona_lisa` as a `var` or 'variable' parameter to a function. If someone at the exhibition vandalized the painting by drawing a moustache onto it, the moustache would still be there when the painting (the `mona_lisa` variable) was returned to the Louvre.

Now let's suppose that the Louvre were to be a bit more cautious. Instead of sending the *original* painting to the exhibition, the museum sends an *exact copy*. That's like a non-`var` or 'value' parameter to a function. This time, the painting is vandalized but the original Mona Lisa remains unchanged. That's because the original painting never left the Louvre. A perfect copy was sent. Changes to the copy do not affect the original. The same is true of value parameters.

Sample Program: Calculating Interest

Let's return to the hypothetical problem we started out with. Let's imagine that we are developing a banking system which needs to calculate the interest payable on various different types of investment account.

Let's assume that our bank offers three types of account: Standard, Silver and Platinum. The Silver account pays one percent more than the Standard rate, and the Gold account pays two percent more. The total interest accrued is calculated as a percentage of the account balance. The bank deducts the same percentages from accounts in debt.

While it would be possible to do these interest calculations separately for each account, this would mean that we'd end up repeating most of the code. When you think about it, you should appreciate that the code needed to calculate the interest for each type of account is essentially the same. Only the percentage rate is different:

It would therefore make better sense to put the calculation routine into its own procedure. If you load up the *interest* project, you'll see that the procedure `CalcInterest` contains the necessary code of the calculation. It also contains an integer variable, `standardRate`, which is assigned the rate of interest that is currently paid on the Standard account:

interest

```
procedure CalcInterest(bonus: integer);
var
    standardRate, balance, intRate: integer;
    intEarned: double;
    msg: string;
begin
    standardRate := 5;
    intRate := standardRate + bonus;
    balance := CurrentBalance;
    intEarned := (balance * intRate) / 100;
    if intEarned < 0 then
        msg := 'Interest deducted from this account is: '
    else
        msg := 'Interest earned on this account is: ';
    Form1.CalcLabel.Caption := msg + FloatToStrF(intEarned, ffCurrency, 2, 2);
end;
```

This means that, if the interest rate changes, we won't have to hunt around in our code making changes in numerous different places. We will only need to alter the value assigned to the `standardRate` variable in this procedure.

The `CalcInterest` procedure takes a single integer parameter, `bonus`, that is used to specify any percentage over and above the Standard rate. It adds this value to the standard rate and assigns this to another variable, `intRate`:

```
intRate :=  standardRate + bonus;
```

It is this new variable which is actually used when calculating the interest payable on an account:

```
intEarned := (balance * intRate) / 100;
```

When you run the program, you can use the scroll bar to select a sum of money (the balance) and click one of the three buttons to see how much interest would be earned:

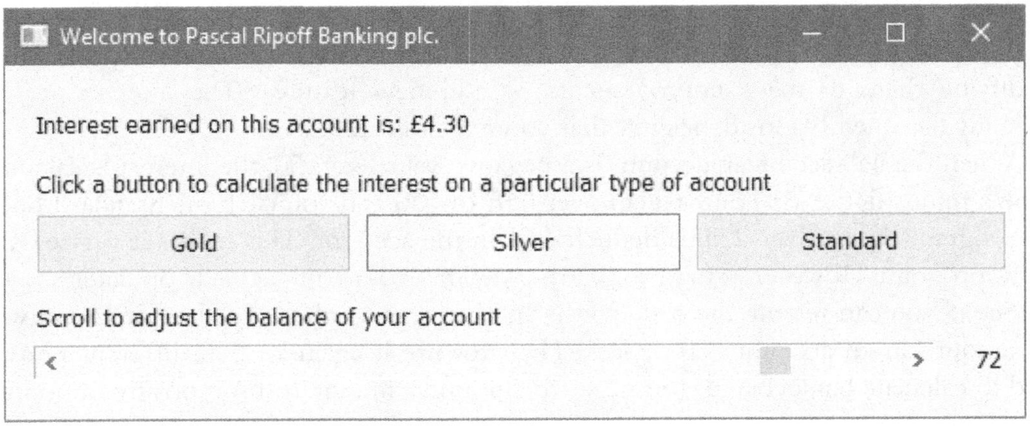

When you want to know the interest payable on a certain balance in each type of account, the code calls call the `CalcInterest` procedure and passes to it an integer value representing the percentage above the Standard rate of interest. For example, the Gold account pays 2 per cent extra, so when the Gold button on the form is clicked, the code in the button-click event handler method calls the `CalcInterest` procedure as follows:

```
CalcInterest(2);
```

The Silver account pays 1 per cent extra and the Standard account does not pay any extra, so these call the `CalcInterest` procedure with the values 1 and 0 respectively. Since all the calculating is done in the `CalcInterest` function, the click-event handlers for the three buttons are extremely simple:

```
procedure TForm1.GoldButtonClick(Sender: TObject);
begin
    CalcInterest(2);
end;

procedure TForm1.SilverButtonClick(Sender: TObject);
begin
    CalcInterest(1);
end;

procedure TForm1.StandardButtonClick(Sender: TObject);
begin
    CalcInterest(0);
end;
```

A Programming Exercise

As you follow this book, I encourage you to play around with my sample programs by modifying them to make improvements or add new features. The interest program currently has one obvious deficiency that you may want to fix.

When the balance of an account is a negative value, say -50, the interest is calculated to be a minus figure. So you have an overdraft of -50 and you click the Standard button the program shows that -2.50 is deducted from the account. This makes it very easy for me to program. However, it may not be the way that your bank actually operates.

See if you can rewrite the code so that no interest is either added or deducted when the amount in an account is 0 or less. Then rewrite it again so that different rates are used to calculate bank charges (on negative amounts) and interest (on positive amounts).

Chapter 4 – Types and Operators

All program data has a type. You need to know the data type in order to do operations upon the data. That's what this chapter is all about.

Solve these two problems:

1. Subtract 1.0 from 2 and add 10 to '53'.
2. Subtract an orange from two grapefruits and add 10 to Shakespeare's Sonnet Number 53?

At first glance you might think that *Problem 1* is easy but *Problem 2* is impossible. In fact, it turns out that the two problems are equally insoluble since each requires that you do arithmetic with incompatible data types: oranges and grapefruits or a floating point (`1.0`) and an integer (`2`); a Sonnet and a number or a string (`'53'`) and an integer (`10`).

Types

Let's look at these problems from a programmer's perspective. Load up the *problem* project. The code of the principal procedure, `DoProblem`, is shown below:

problem

```
procedure DoProblem;
var
    num1                : double;
    num2, x, total      : integer;
    s, sonnetnum        : string;
begin
    num1      := 1.0;
    num2      := 2;
    x         := 10;
    sonnetnum := '53';
    total     :=  num2 - num1;
    s         :=  sonnetnum + x;
    ShowResults(total, s);
end;
```

When you try to run this program, you will immediately run into trouble. The compiler stops on this line:

```
total := num2 - num1;
```

It displays an error message stating that the types are incompatible. It might not be immediately obvious what the problem is. After all, both the variables used in the calculation have been given valid numeric values earlier in the procedure:

```
num1 := 1.0;
num2 := 2;
```

Number Types

So why can't we simply subtract the value of `num1` (`1.0`) from the value of `num2` (`2`) and assign the result to the variable, `total`? The answer can be found in the variable declaration section, beneath the keyword `var` at the top of the `DoProblem` procedure:

```
var
    num1                : double;
    num2, x, total      : integer;
    s, sonnetnum        : string;
```

Here you can see that the variables `total` and `num2` are both declared as integers. These are whole numbers with no fractional part. But the variable `num1` is a `double`, which is a floating-point number.

In effect, this code tries to do a floating-point calculation (`2 - 1.0`) and assign the value to an `integer` variable. As far as the compiler is concerned, this cannot be done. Even though the `double` variable currently has a whole-number value, 1.0, it is conceivable that this value could be changed during the execution of the program, say to 1.666. If that were to happen it would be impossible to assign a meaningful result to the `integer` variable, `total`. The compiler takes the view that it is better to be safe than sorry and so it demands that we use compatible data types at the outset.

To fix this code, edit the declaration of `num1` by changing its type from `double` to `integer`, like this:

```
num1 : integer;
```

Now try running the program again. This time the compiler stops on this assignment:

```
num1 := 1.0;
```

Now that `num1` is an integer, we can't assign to it a floating point value. Change this to:

```
num1 := 1;
```

This time, when you try to run the code, the compiler stops at:

```
s := sonnetnum + x;
```

The reason for this problem should be easy to spot. The variables, `s`, and `sonnetnum` are declared to be of the `string` type, but `x` is declared to be an `integer`. You may recall that the `+` operator can be used either with numbers or with strings. Let's try converting `x` to a `string`. Delete the declaration of `x` and declare it as a `string`. The `var` section should now look like this:

```
var
    num1              : integer;
    num2,total        : integer;
    x, s, sonnetnum   : string;
```

Make sure that the value assigned to `x` is a `string` by enclosing it between single-quotes:

```
x := '10';
```

When you run the program now all the data types are compatible and so the compilation should proceed without error. At the end of it all, a window will pop up containing a single button. Click the button to display the results of the calculations. This shows that the first calculation (`2 - 1`), produces the expected result, `1`. However, the second calculation (`'53' + '10'`), does not result in `63` but in `'5310'`:

The reason for this is that, when used with strings, the `+` operator adds the second string, here `'10'` (that is, the two characters `'1'` and `'0'`), onto the end of the first string: `'53'`.

Strings and Numbers

The fact that these characters happen to *look* like numbers is irrelevant. As far as the computer program is concerned, a string is made up of a sequence of characters, each of which has the `char` data-type. You cannot do arithmetical calculations with characters. The fix for this problem is to declare both `x` and `sonnetnum` as integers. The `var` declaration section should now look something like this:

```
var
    num1,
    num2,
    x,
    sonnetnum,
    total: integer;
    s: string;
```

Edit their assignments too, by removing the single quote characters to turn the value from strings to integers:

```
x := 10;
sonnetnum := 53;
```

This, however, provides us with one more problem. We can only display strings on screen, not integers. The `ShowMessage` procedure requires a `string` parameter, so how can we persuade it to display our integer results?

We've already encountered this problem in previous programs so you probably won't be surprised to discover that, once again, the solution is provided by the `IntToStr` function which takes an integer argument and returns its string representation. If you scroll up the code, you will see that `IntToStr` is used in the `ShowResults` procedure:

```
procedure ShowResults(total: integer; s: string);
begin
    ShowMessage(IntToStr(total) + '    ' + s);
end;
```

We can use the same function in the `DoProblem` procedure to convert the result of our integer calculation (`sonnetnum + x`) prior to assigning the value to the `string` variable, `s`. You can edit the assignment as follows:

```
s := IntToStr(sonnetnum + x);
```

Check that the edited procedure now exactly matches the rewritten code shown on the next page (or you can comment out the original procedure and uncomment the revised version in the source code):

```
procedure DoProblem;
var
    num1, num2,
    x, sonnetnum,
    total      : integer;
    s          : string;
begin
    num1       := 1;
    num2       := 2;
    x          := 10;
    sonnetnum  := 53;
    total      :=  num2 - num1;
    s          :=  IntToStr(sonnetnum + x);
    ShowResults(total, s);
end;
```

Run the program again and click the button. You should see that the two results are now correct: 1 and 63:

Before we finally leave this subject, you might like to consider these problems:

1. Add '10' to the first line of Shakespeare's Sonnet 53.
2. Add 10 to the first line of Shakespeare's Sonnet 53.

Given my discussion of types and type-conversion, you should see that these conundrums are not quite as ridiculous they first appear. See if you can write a program that finds a different solution to each of the two problems. Here are two additional pieces of information you will need:

- The first line of Sonnet 53 is: *'What is your substance, whereof are you made'*
- To find the length of a string use the `Length` function.

This is a simple example using `Length` with the `string` variable, `s`:

```
Length(s);
```

Once you've written your own program, check your code against my solution, which you'll find in the *sonnet* project.

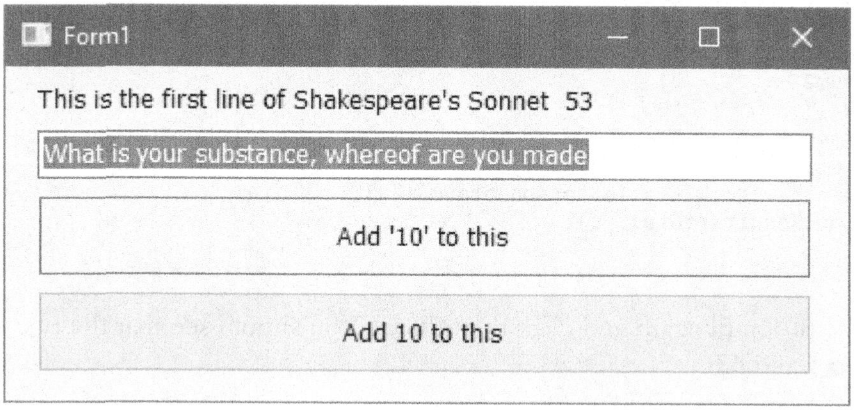

Length function or Length property?

Strings in Delphi have a `Length` property so you can obtain the length of a `string` variable `s` and assign that value to the `integer` variable `len` like this:

```
len := s.Length;
```

However, even though the `Text` of an Edit box can, in most respects be used like any other string, it is actually declared to be a type of `TCaption` object which does not have a `Length` property. That is why I use the `Length` *function* here. I'll have more to say about properties in Chapter 8.

Parameters and Type Checking

To help familiarize yourself with some other important standard types, load and run the *types* project. When you click the top or the bottom button, some data is displayed in a label right above the buttons. When you click the middle button, the value of a `Boolean` variable is toggled between `true` and `false` (as mentioned earlier, `true` or `false` are the only two possible values of a `Boolean`):

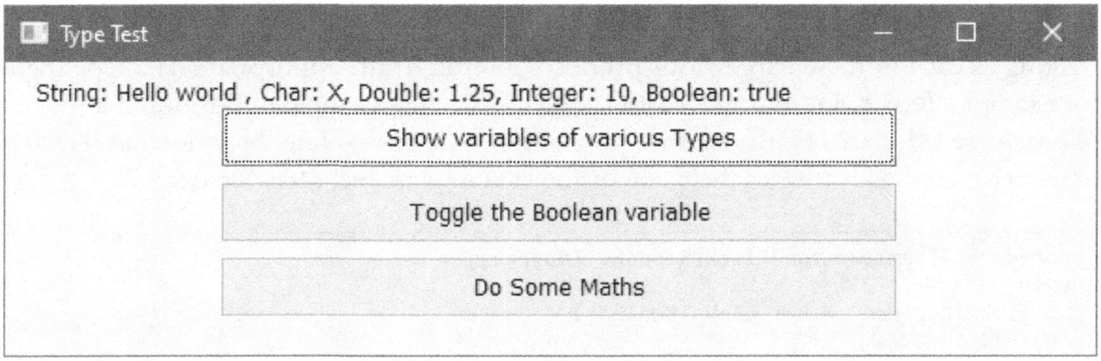

If you take a look at the code, you will see that the label's text (its `Caption` property) is set by the procedure `TForm1.Showall` which takes five arguments in this order:
[1] `string`, [2] `char`, [3] `double`, [4] `integer`, [5] `string`:

types

```
procedure TForm1.Showall(s: string; c: char; d: double; i: integer; s2: string);
var
    resultStr: string;
begin
    resultStr := 'String: ' + s + ', Char: ' + c + ', Double: ' + FloatToStr(d)
      + ', Integer: ' + IntToStr(i) + ', Boolean: ' + s2;
    ResultLbl.Caption := resultStr;
end;
```

Both *Button1* and *Button3* pass data items to be displayed by this procedure. `Button1Click` declares four variables of the appropriate types and passes them as the first four arguments to the `ShowAll` procedure. I'll explain the fifth argument, `BoolStr`, in a moment:

```
Showall(myString, myChar, myDouble, myInteger, BoolStr);
```

Each data item (or 'argument') passed to the procedure must match the type and position of the named variable (or 'parameter') declared in the procedure itself, otherwise the code will not compile.

`Button3Click` also passes a set of parameters of the correct data type. However, you will see that this time, in addition to variables, I've also included some mathematical expressions (e.g. `10.0 * d`):

```
ShowAll('10 * 100 ', c, 10.0 * d , 10 * i , BoolStr);
```

As long as each of these expressions produces a result of the appropriate data type (here, for example, `10.0 * d` results in a `double`, which is what is required at position 3 in the list of parameters declared by the `Showall` procedure), then that is fine. Now look at the code of `Button2Click`. This toggles the value of the `Boolean` variable, `globalBoolean`:

```
procedure TForm1.Button2Click(Sender: TObject);
begin
    globalBoolean := not globalBoolean;
end;
```

Logical Negation

In Pascal, `not` is the 'logical negation operator'. In effect it returns the opposite of a `Boolean` value. So the expression `not true` returns `false` whereas the expression `not false` returns `true`. Here the value returned from the expression `not globalBoolean` is assigned back to the `globalBoolean` variable itself. This means that the expression `globalBoolean := not globalBoolean` has the effect of toggling the `globalBoolean` variable between `true` and `false`.

Global and Local Variables

The `globalBoolean` variable has been declared in the `var` section toward the top of the code unit, just above the keyword `implementation`. Its declaration here makes it available to all the procedures and functions in the unit:

```
var
    Form1: TForm1;
    globalBoolean: boolean;
```

This contrasts with those variables declared in the `var` sections of individual procedures. These 'local' variables are visible only within (or 'local' to) procedure in which they are declared. They are not available to code outside that procedure. For example, the variables `myDouble`, `myInteger`, `myChar` and `myString` are available to the code inside the `TForm1.Button1Click` procedure but not in any other procedure:

```
procedure TForm1.Button1Click(Sender: TObject);
var
    myDouble: double;
    myInteger: integer;
    myChar: char;
    myString: string;
```

Local and Global Scope

'Scope' describes the 'visibility' of variables and other pieces of code. For a more detailed discussion of this, see the section on '*Scope*' later in this chapter.

The problem with the various numeric data types used in this project is that I want to be able to display their values in the label on the form. A label can only display strings, not numbers. So each piece of numeric data has to be 'translated' into a string in order to be displayed. Look again at the parameters declared by `Showall`:

```
procedure TForm1.Showall(s: string; c: char; d: double; i: integer; s2: string);
```

The first parameter presents no problem since it is a string already. The second parameter, which is a `char` (a 'character'), presents no difficulties either. Recall that a string is just a series of characters 'strung' together and a `char` can be added to the end of a string. But the third and fourth parameters are both numeric data types – a `double` and an `integer` – and so these must be specifically converted to their string representations before they can be displayed in the label. I can use the `IntToStr` function to return the string version of a whole number and the `FloatToStr` function to return the string version of a floating point number such as a double. You'll see that these functions are used in the `ShowAll` procedure:

```
FloatToStr(d)
IntToStr(i)
```

Booleans

The final item in the `ShowAll` procedure's parameter list, `s2`, looks as though it should be straightforward since it's another string. However, the two button-click procedures, `Button1Click` and `Button3Click`, want to display the value of a `Boolean` variable at this position. I have written a simple function to return the string representation of a `Boolean`:

```
function TForm1.BoolStr : string;
begin
    if (globalBoolean) then
        BoolStr := 'true'
    else
        BoolStr := 'false';
end;
```

This function simply uses an `if` test to determine the current value of the `Boolean` variable, `globalBoolean` and returns a string, `'true'` or `'false'`, as appropriate. Note that, since a `true` value necessarily evaluates to `true` it is not necessary to make an explicit test using the equality operator, like this:

```
if (globalBoolean = true) then
```

The test shown above works but it's not needed. When you perform an `if` test, you are testing the value *returned* by an expression. That value is always `Boolean` – either `true` or `false` so when testing a `Boolean` variable, you only need to put the variable itself as the test condition like this: `if (globalBoolean)`

In my code, the `BoolStr` function is itself passed as the fifth argument to `ShowAll` by the two button-click procedures:

```
ShowAll(myString, myChar, myDouble, myInteger, BoolStr);
ShowAll('10 * 100 ', c, 10.0 * d , 10 * i , BoolStr);
```

When a function name is given as an argument, what actually happens is that the function is called and it is the value that is returned from that function that is passed as the actual argument (just so long as the return type of the function matches the expected argument type). In the `ShowAll` function-calls above, it is the string value returned from the `BoolStr` function which is passed as the fifth argument to `ShowAll`.

BoolToStr

You don't have to write your own function to translate a `Boolean` into a string representation, as I have. Delphi provides a conversion function named `BoolToStr`. If you specify a `Boolean` value as a single argument to this function the string representation returned will be (rather bizarrely!) `'-1'` for `true` and `'0'` for `false`. In order to make it return more descriptive strings, you need to pass a `true` value as a second argument. Look at these examples.

If `globalBoolean` is `true`, the code shown below returns `'-1'`. If `globalBoolean` is `false`, it returns `'0'`:

```
BoolToStr(globalBoolean);
```

But now I pass `true` as the second argument. In this case, if `globalBoolean` is `true`, this returns `'True'`. If `globalBoolean` is `false`, it returns `'False'`:

```
BoolToStr(globalBoolean, true);
```

Frankly, I think I'll stick to my own simpler `BoolStr` function!

Mathematical Operators

In this book, I have already used operators to add, subtract and multiply values. Pascal, in common with other computer languages, provides various arithmetic operators which are shown below:

Operator	**Purpose**
`+`	addition
`-`	subtraction
`*`	multiplication
`/`	division
`div`	integer division
`mod`	modulus

The first three operators shown above (`+`, `-`, `*`) can be used both with whole numbers such as the `integer` and with floating-point types such as `double`. The final three operators are type-specific, however. The division operator `/` results in a floating-point number whereas the `div` operator results in an integer number. An integer division such as 10 divided by 3 may, of course, leave a remainder. The `mod` operator returns this remainder. For example, the expressions shown below would produce the results shown alongside:

Expression	Result
`10 / 3`	3.33333333333333
`10 div 3`	3
`10 mod 3`	1

A few examples of these operators are provided in the *ops* sample project.

Scope

You may have noticed in the sample programs that some variables have been declared towards the top of a unit while others have been declared inside individual procedures.

Although it is often possible to declare a variable in one or more places, you would be wrong to think that the location of its declaration is of no consequence. A variable declared in one place may have a different effect (possibly an unintentional side-effect) from a variable declared in another place. That's because the place in which a variable is declared defines the 'visibility' or 'scope' of that variable.

Visibility of Variables

The 'scope' of a variable is the part of the program in which that variable can be used. Variables declared inside a procedure have a scope that is 'local' to that procedure. Local variables are not available *outside* the procedure in which they are declared. On the other hand, variables declared at the top of a unit, are available to all the code in that unit.

Local Variables

Load up the *types* project and look at the source code. You will see that two sets of variables have been declared, beneath the `var` keyword, one set inside the click-handling procedure, `Button1Click` and another set inside `Button3Click`. Here, is the code of these two procedures:

```
types
procedure TForm1.Button1Click(Sender: TObject);
var
    myDouble : double;
    myInteger : integer;
    myChar : char;
    myString : string;
begin
    myString := 'Hello world ';
    myChar := 'X';
    myDouble := 1.25;
    myInteger := 10;
    ShowAll(myString, myChar, myDouble, myInteger, BoolStr);
    BoolToStr(globalBoolean, true));
end;

procedure TForm1.Button3Click(Sender: TObject);
var
    i : integer;
    d : double;
    c : char;
begin
    d := 100.0;
    i := 100;
    c := '$';
    ShowAll('10 * 100 ', c, 10.0 * d , 10 * i , BoolStr);
end;
```

The `Button2Click` procedure does not declare any variables. However, it assigns a value to a `Boolean` variable called `globalBoolean`. It uses the `not` operator, to toggle the `Boolean` value:

```
procedure TForm1.Button2Click(Sender: TObject);
begin
    globalBoolean := not globalBoolean;
end;
```

Unlike the other variables in this program, `globalBoolean`, is not declared in the `var` section of a specific procedure. To find its declaration you need to scroll up to find the `var` section just above the keyword `implementation`:

```
var
    Form1: TForm1;
    globalBoolean : boolean;
implementation
```

Why, you may wonder, has this variable been singled out in this way? The answer is summarized in one import word – *scope*. I want the variable to be available to all the code in all the procedures in the entire unit. In other words, I want its scope to be 'global' rather than 'local'.

Global Variables

To be technically accurate, a variable with 'global' scope is one that is available throughout an entire program (which might contain many different source code units). As this program contains just one code unit, you may regard `globalBoolean` as being, to all intents and purposes, 'global'.

You can verify that this variable is accessible everywhere by running the program and clicking the middle button, *Button2*, a few times. After each click, press either *Button1* or *Button3*. You will find that the `Boolean` value at the end of the list of variables displayed in the label, has been changed by the `Button2Click` procedure. The `Boolean` variable, `globalBoolean`, is available to all three `ButtonClick` procedures so if one procedure (here the `Button2Click` procedure) changes its value, then its value remains changed in the other procedures too.

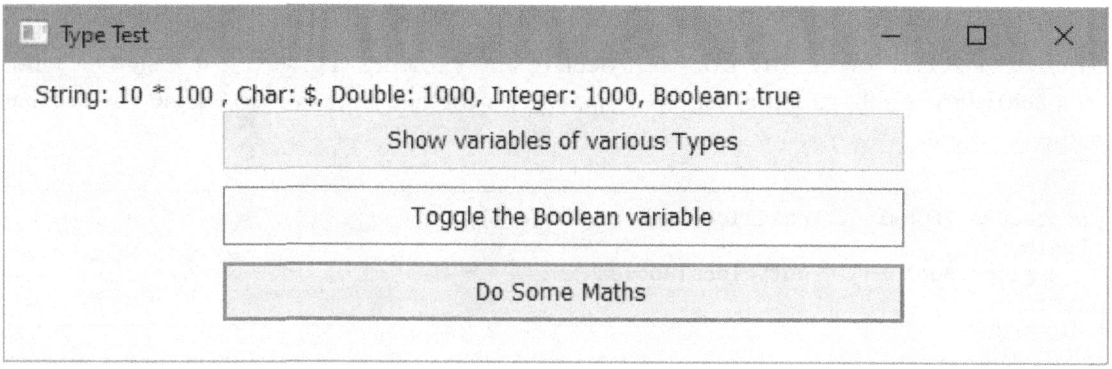

Now let's consider what happens to the local variables declared inside individual procedures. For example, look at `Button1Click`. Among other variables, this declares a string called `myString` and it assigns to it the value `'Hello world'`. We've already verified that the *global* variable, `globalBoolean`, remains in existence throughout the lifetime of this application. How long, then, is the lifetime of a *local* variable such as `myString`?

It turns out that local variables only exist for as long as the procedure in which they are declared is running. When *Button1* is clicked, the `Button1Click` procedure starts to run. The local variables declared in its `var` section pop into existence and they continue to exist as long as the procedure continues to run. But as soon as the procedure has finished running (that is, when the program's execution passes beyond the final `end;` marker of the procedure), the local variables pop out of existence again.

You might find it difficult to imagine things popping into and out of existence in this way. After all, it's not the kind of thing that happens much in the real world. It is the kind of thing that happens in science-fiction, however. Indeed, in the fictional world of the Star Trek TV universe, it happens all the time.

Variables on the Holodeck

When a crew member of the Starship Enterprise wants to relax, he or she can step into a computer-generated holographic world on the Holodeck. When a person enters the Holodeck, all kinds of holographic items instantly pop into existence. These items remain in existence just so long as the crew member stays on the Holodeck. When a person leaves the Holodeck, the computer-generated items pop out of existence again.

Load and run the *trek* program. When you click the button labelled *'Go To Holodeck'*, you'll see that you have two weapons - a HoloWeapon called 'Inverse Verteron Pulse Beam' and a Real Weapon called 'Phaser Gun'.

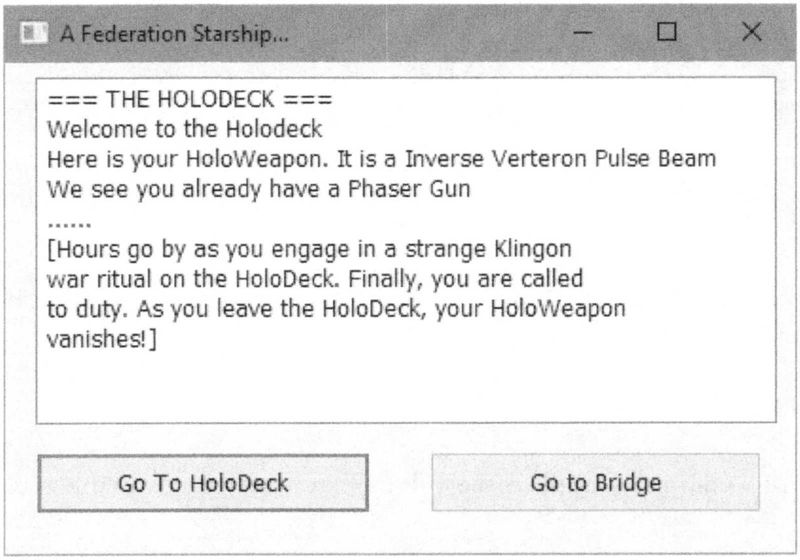

But when you click the button labelled *'Go To Bridge'*, you no longer have the HoloWeapon. You only have the Phaser Gun.

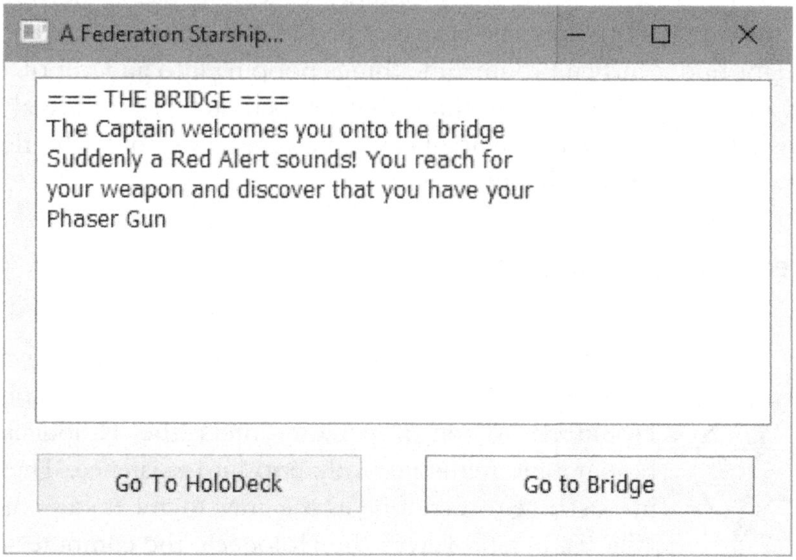

This is more than just a trick. This is a true representation of what is going on in the program itself. The HoloWeapon only exists inside the `GoToHoloDeck` procedure. If the program is still running, stop it. Now double-click the button labelled *'Go To Holodeck'*. In the source code editor, you can see that `Button1Click` calls the `GoToHolodeck` procedure. This procedure declares a variable called `holoWeapon` which is local to the procedure and it assigns to that variable the string: `'Inverse Verteron Pulse Beam'`:

Trek

```
procedure TForm1.GoToHoloDeck;
var
    holoWeapon: string;
begin
    holoWeapon := 'Inverse Verteron Pulse Beam';
```

You can easily check that this variable still exists later in the procedure by displaying its name in the `Memo1` component on the form:

```
Memo1.Lines.Add('Here is your HoloWeapon. It is a ' + holoWeapon);
```

Notice that the procedure also displays the value of another string variable, `realWeapon`:

```
Memo1.Lines.Add('We see you already have a ' + realWeapon);
```

The `realWeapon` variable is not declared within the procedure itself. Scroll further up the *Starship.pas* unit and you'll see that `realWeapon` has been declared in the code unit's `var` section:

```
var
    Form1: TForm1;
    realWeapon: string;
```

So `realWeapon` exists, and can be used by code, throughout the *Starship* unit, whereas `holoWeapon` only pops into existence when the program enters the `GoToHolodeck` procedure. It pops out of existence again when the program exits the `GoToHoloDeck` procedure.

This is precisely what happens in the fictional universe of Star Trek too. Captain Picard has his real weapon, a Phaser Gun, wherever he happens to be on the Enterprise. It is with him both on the Bridge and on the Holodeck.

However, let's imagine that he now goes to the Holodeck to brush up his Klingon battle skills. When he enters the Holodeck, the computer provides him with a holographic weapon, which in this case happens to be an Inverse Verteron Pulse Beam. As long as he stays on the Holodeck, he has both a Phaser Gun and an Inverse Verteron Pulse Beam.

When he leaves the Holodeck, however, the holographic weapon disappears and he is left with only the real weapon, his Phaser Gun. In other words, the Phaser Gun has *global* scope – it exists everywhere in the Starship. But the Inverse Verteron Pulse Beam has *local* scope – it pops into existence when the Holodeck is entered and it pops out of existence again when the Holodeck is exited.

If you want to check that the local `holoWeapon` variable really does not exist outside the `GoToHoloDeck` procedure, remove the `//` comment characters from this line in the `TForm1.GoToBridge` procedure, which executes when you click the second button on the form:

```
//  Memo1.Lines.Add(holoWeapon);
```

The line should now appear as:

```
Memo1.Lines.Add(holoWeapon);
```

Now run the program again. The compiler will stop on this line and an error message warning of an unknown or undeclared identifier will appear in the Messages window.

The identifier, `holoWeapon`, is unknown due to the fact that it only exists within the scope of the `TForm1.GoToHoloDeck` procedure. In the `TForm1.GoToBridge` procedure, the variable does not exist. On the other hand, the global variable, `realWeapon`, is within the scope of the entire *Starship* unit so it is available within this procedure. The scope of the two procedures and the unit is represented in this diagram:

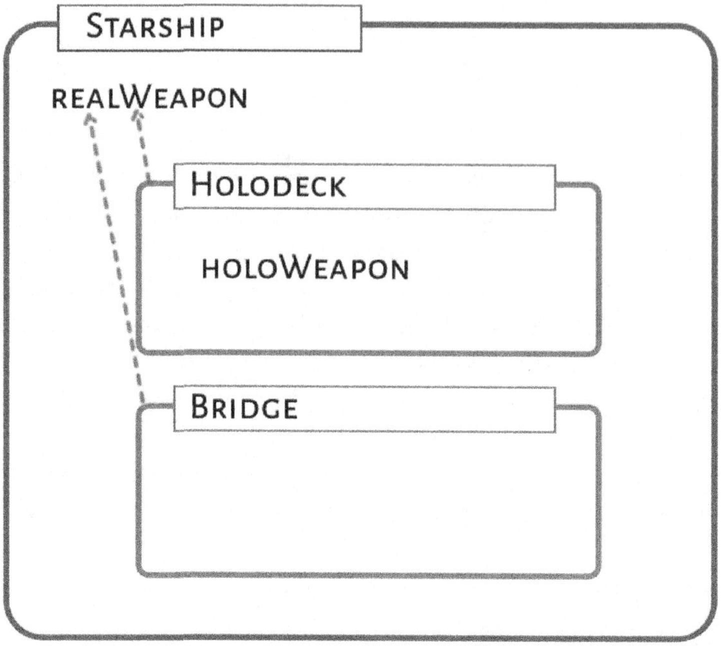

Think of the Holodeck and the Bridge as two unconnected rooms. Each room can contain items that are not available anywhere else in the Starship. So `holoWeapon` is only available in the Holodeck but not on the Bridge or anywhere else.

However, items stored outside the rooms, somewhere in the 'global' scope of the Starship are available everywhere – so `realWeapon` is available on the Bridge and also in the Holodeck.

In my program `Starship` is a unit in which a global variable `realWeapon` is declared. The two procedures `GoToBridge` and `GoToHolodeck` can access the `realWeapon` variable. But the `GoToHolodeck` procedure cannot access the `holoWeapon` variable which is declared in the `GoToHolodeck` procedure.

Same Name, Different Scope?

As you would expect, *you cannot have a two variables with the same name within the* same *scope*. That would be a recipe for disaster. You cannot declare two global variables like this:

```
realWeapon,
realWeapon : string;
```

If you try this, the compiler will stop with the error message warning of a duplicate identifier. On the other hand, *you can use the same variable name in* different *scopes*. Load up the *testvars* project to see how this is done.

Look first at the `ButtonClick` procedures for *Button1* and *Button2*. Each of these declares a local variable, `i`, and assigns it a different value: 10 or 20. The procedure then displays the value of `i` in the *Edit* box:

testvars

```
procedure TForm1.Button1Click(Sender: TObject);
var
    i : integer;
begin
    i := 10;
    Edit1.Text := IntToStr(i);
end;

procedure TForm1.Button2Click(Sender: TObject);
var
    i : integer;
begin
    i := 20;
    Edit1.Text := IntToStr(i);
end;
```

There is no problem with using the same variable name inside each of the two procedures. Since each variable only comes into existence when a procedure is run, there is no possibility of confusing one variable with another of the same name and so the compiler doesn't complain about duplicate identifiers. Now look at `Button3Click`:

```
procedure TForm1.Button3Click(Sender: TObject);
begin
    i := 30;
    Edit1.Text := IntToStr(i);
end;
```

This procedure also assigns a value to a variable named `i`. However, unlike the other two procedures, the `Button3Click` procedure does not declare a local variable called `i`. If you scroll to the `var` section just above the keyword `implementation`, you will find that a *global* variable named `i` is declared here:

```
var
    Form1: TForm1;
    i : integer;
```

This is the only variable named `i` which is within the scope of `Button3Click`. Remember, a procedure inside a unit has access to variables within the 'scope' of that unit. Clearly, then, this global variable `i` must be the one that is used within the `Button3Click` procedure.

But, the existence of the global variable `i` poses an important question: which variable `i` is being assigned a value in each of the other two procedures, `Button1Click` and `Button2Click`? Within these procedures, two variables called `i` are available - the *global* variable `i` and the *local* variable `i`.

To see which variables are actually assigned values by these procedures, run the *testvars* program. Now follow these steps:

- Click *Button3*, the one labelled *'Set i to 30'*. Remember, there is no local variable `i` in the `Button3Click` procedure.
- Click the *'Test i'* button to display the value of the global variable `i`. As expected *Button3* has set it to 30.
- Now click *Button1*, labelled *'Set i to 10'*. This procedure includes a *local* variable `i`.
- Click *'Test i'* once again. The value of the *global* `i` is still 30.

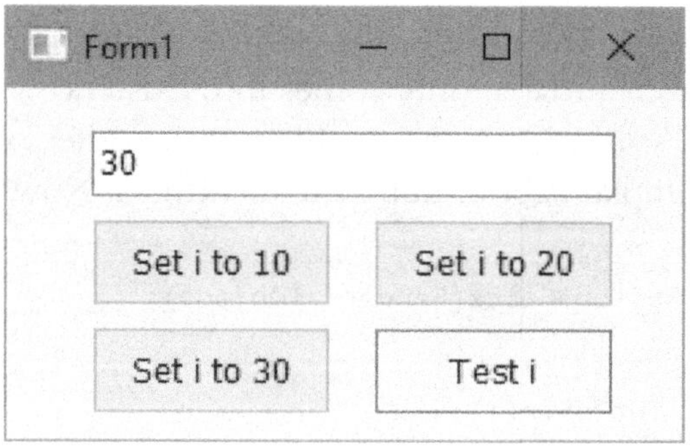

In other words, *Button1*'s local variable `i` takes precedence over the global variable `i`. It is a general rule of Pascal, and most other programming languages, that the innermost scope is given precedence. So a local variable will always be used in preference to a global variable of the same name.

Variables with the Same Names

Giving the same name to local and global variables (or any variables which share a 'scope') may lead to confusion and could cause unexpected side-effects and program bugs. The more global, or 'unit-level' variables you use, the more likely you are to introduce unexpected errors into your programs. For that reason, you should use global and unit-level variables only when there is no alternative. If several procedures need to access the same piece of data, it is usually better to create a local variable and pass it as an argument to other procedures. Only when you are sure that variable must exist continuously throughout the life of your program should it be given global or unit-level scope.

To consolidate your understanding of the scope of variables, run the *scope* project. Click the buttons to see the effect of assigning values to both global and local variables. Pay particular attention to the variables called `aStr` as this name is declared both locally, in `TForm1.Button1Click` and `TForm1.Button2Click`, and also 'globally' in the `var` section above the `implementation` keyword:

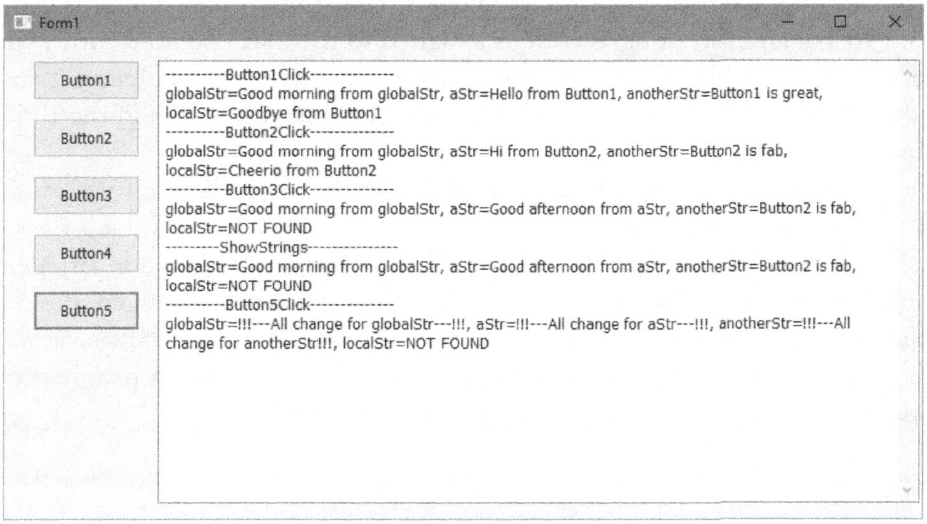

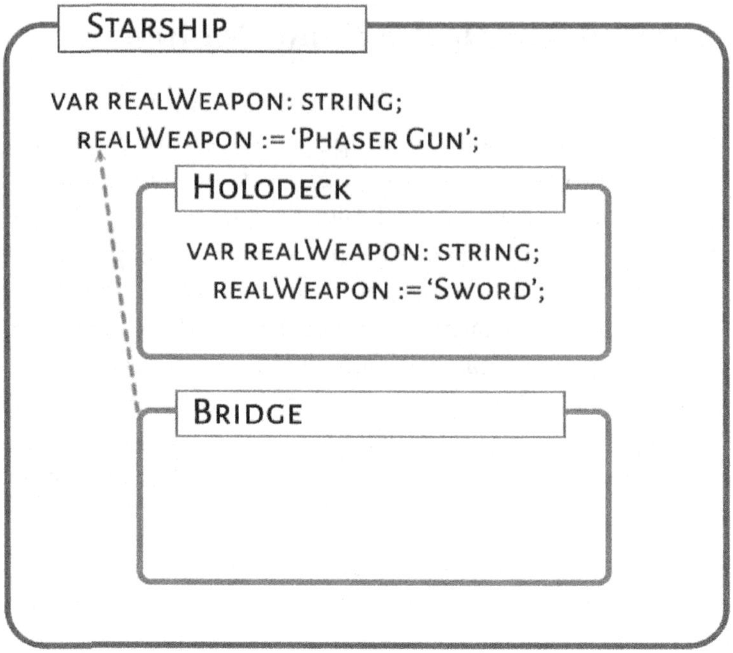

Taking our Star Trek analogy, let's assume that the `realWeapon` variable is declared globally for the Starship and locally for the Holodeck. The string 'Phaser Gun' is assigned to the global variable and the string 'Sword' is assigned to the local variable. Now, whenever any code uses the variable `realWeapon` in the Holodeck (that is, the `Holodeck` *procedure*) its value will be 'Sword'. But when any code uses the variable `realWeapon` in the Bridge procedure, its value will be 'Phaser Gun'.

But what would happen if a new value (let's say the string 'Laser Rifle') were to be assigned to `realWeapon` inside the Holodeck? Would that change the value of `realWeapon` in Bridge? And what would happen if a new string were to be assigned in Bridge? Would that change the value in Holodeck? And if either procedure changed the value of `realWeapon`, would those changes affect its value if a variable called `realWeapon` were then used in a third procedure? If you are unsure about this, try writing a program to test it out. Scope is important so make sure you really understand it!

Chapter 5 – Loops, Arrays and Strings

In this chapter we learn how to automate repetitive tasks by running bits of code repeatedly inside loops.

The world's first robots made their appearance in the 1921 production of Karel Capek's stage play "R.U.R." (Rossum's Universal Robots). The word 'robot' derives from the Czech word 'robota', meaning (approximately) 'compulsory labour'. The perfect robot is happy to carry out mindless repetitive tasks, day-in, day-out, leaving humanity free to enjoy the finer things in life.

Robots are no longer confined to science fiction. These days, most of us have several of them in our own homes. They may not look quite as human-like as the robots in films, but our washing machines, security cameras and dish-washers are robots in the true sense of the word. We tell them what to do by feeding them instructions using a keypad, dial or remote-control unit. And their little silicon-chip brains carry out our commands with unthinking obedience.

In this chapter we are going to find out how to write robot-like computer programs that will carry out tedious, repetitive tasks. We'll even create our own computerized washing machine with a range of selectable wash-and-spin cycles. This may not be quite as exciting as the R2-D2 and C-3PO robots in Star Wars. But at least it's a start…

'for' Loops

First, let's find out how to create a very simple 'program loop' that repeats an action a specific number of times. One of the things every programmer needs is an ASCII table. The acronym, ASCII, stands for American Standard Code for Information Interchange. The alphabetic and numeric characters displayed on your screen may be represented internally by a specific code number in the ASCII table.

ASCII Codes and Characters

Let's look at a few example of ASCII codes. The ASCII code 66 equates to the upper-case 'A' character, whereas ASCII code 97 equates to a lower-case 'a'. There are also ASCII codes for invisible characters such as space (ASCII 32) and Carriage Return (ASCII 13). There is even a backspace character (ASCII 8) which is generated by the backspace key on your keyboard.

It is useful to know all the available ASCII values in order to be able to manipulate the characters in strings. For example, you could perform arithmetical operations using ASCII values in order to encrypt the characters in a password. There are 128 characters in the standard ASCII table numbered from 0 to 127 and there are 256 characters in the 'extended' ASCII table numbered from 0 to 255.

UTF Characters

These days the UTF-8 (Unicode Transformation Format) character set is often used in preference to ASCII as this represents a larger range of characters, which is convenient for representing international characters and special symbols. The first 128 characters in UTF-8 set character set are the same as those in ASCII.

One way of printing the character equivalent of each ASCII code would be to write 256 statements, one for each character. Using the Object Pascal dot-notation syntax, you could then display each number and character on a line in a list box. To print the upper-case alphabet in a ListBox we would need 26 lines, one each for ASCII codes 65 ('A') to 90 ('Z'):

```
ListBox1.Items.Add('Ascii 65 = ' + Chr(65));
ListBox1.Items.Add('Ascii 66 = ' + Chr(66));
  { insert 23 more lines of code here! }
ListBox1.Items.Add('Ascii 90 = ' + Chr(90));
```

That would certainly work. But it would take a lot of time and effort to write all the code needed to display the entire alphabet, one character at a time. It would be much simpler and quicker if only we could tell the program to count from 65 to 90 or from 0 to 255 and display the characters matching all of those ASCII codes. Fortunately, we can do that very easily.

Load up the *ascii* project. This uses a simple form onto which I have placed a list box called `ListBox1`. Here all the code I've used to display the ASCII table:

ascii

```
procedure TForm1.FormCreate(Sender: TObject);
var
    i : integer;
begin
    for i := 0 to 255 do
        ListBox1.Items.Add('Ascii ' + IntToStr(i) + ' = ' + Chr(i));
end;
```

In effect, this code compresses 256 statements into just two lines. And it's all down to that simple word, `for`. The code sets up a loop of execution that continues running as long as the value of the variable `i` falls between 0 and 255. Each time the loop executes, 1 is added to the value of `i`.

Properties

When referring to visual objects such as *ListBox* or *Label,* you must be sure to use the appropriate 'dot-notation'. For example, this is how you would append *'Hello world'* to the caption of a label named *Label1*:

```
Label1.Caption := Label1.Caption + 'Hello world';
```

Here `Caption` is said to be a 'property' of the `Label1` object. If you drop a `Label` onto a form in the Form Design environment, you will see that `Caption` is shown in the Properties panel. You can set properties using this panel while in the Form Designer or you can set properties in code by making an assignment just as I assigned a string to the `Label1.Caption` property above. Properties are explained in more detail in Chapter 8.

UTF-8 Conversion

If the code in the *ascii* project does not display the characters of the extended ASCII codes (in my tests Delphi does display them but Lazarus does not) you may need to convert the characters explicitly to UTF-8. To do that, comment out this line:

```
ListBox1.Items.Add('Ascii ' + IntToStr(i) + ' = ' + Chr(i));
```

Use this line instead:

```
ListBox1.Items.Add('Ascii ' + IntToStr(i) + ' = ' + UTF8Encode(String(Chr(i))));
```

The code has been placed into the `TForm1.FormCreate` procedure (this was created automatically by clicking *OnCreate* in the Events page of the Object Inspector). This procedure executes when the application is first run.

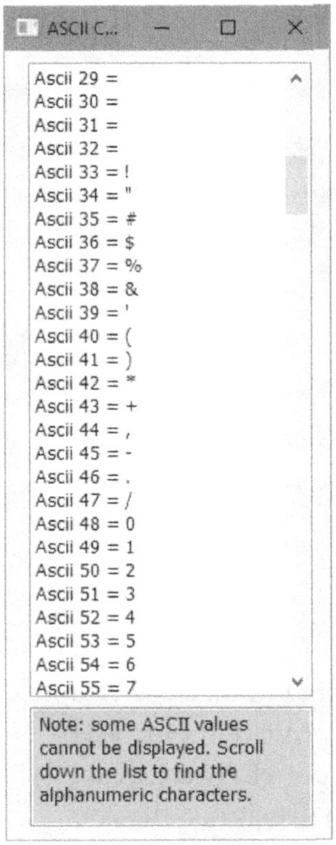

In this case a single line of code follows the declaration of the `for` loop so only that line is executed each time through the loop. If you want to execute several lines of code with each pass through the loop, you would need to place them between the keywords `begin` and `end`.

char/integer Conversion

Incidentally, notice that I've used two type-conversion conversion functions here, each of which displays the value of `i` on each pass through the loop. I've used the `IntToStr` function many times before. It converts an integer variable to its string representation. So if `i` equals 65 then `IntToStr(i)` returns the string '65'.

The `Chr` function is rather different. This returns a *character* equivalent of an *integer* value. So if `i` equals 65 then `Chr(i)` returns 'A' which is the character equivalent of ASCII code 65. The complementary function to `Chr` is `Ord` which converts a character to its ASCII value. For example, `Ord('A')` returns the integer value, 65.

Non-visible Characters

As you will have seen (or *not* seen!), the first 31 characters in the ASCII table are not displayed on screen – they are 'non-printing characters'. The 32nd character *is* displayed but you won't see much since it is a space character.

Let's suppose that you want to omit the invisible characters from the chart. Let's assume you want to categorize the remaining characters by labelling them to indicate whether they are letters, numbers or some other kind of 'special' character.

By examining the ASCII chart, you can figure out that the codes can be divided into categories as follows (note that the characters in the upper reaches, above 127, of the 'extended' ASCII table may vary depending on the font being used and which international settings are active on your computer).

For my purposes, if a character is not an alphabetic or numeric character, I will regard it as some sort of 'special' character.

ASCII CODES	CHARACTERS	CATEGORY
65..90	'A' to 'Z'	Letters
97..122	'a' to 'z'	Letters
48..57	'0' to '9'	Numbers
33..47	'!' to '/'	Special
58..64	':' to '@'	Special
91..96	'[' to '`'	Special
123..255	'{' to 'ÿ'	Special

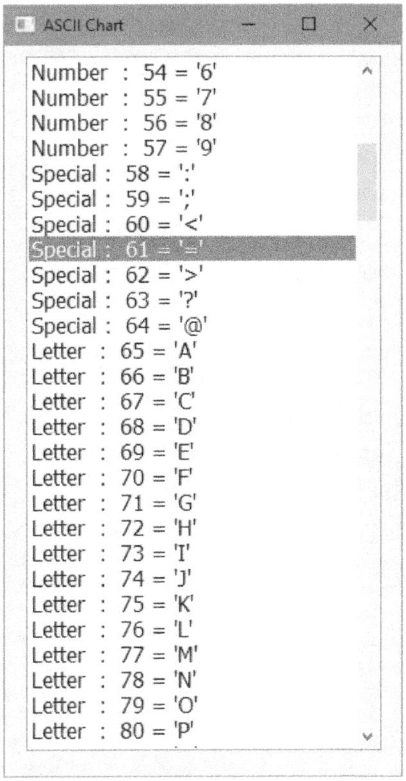

Try to think how you would you go about re-programming the ASCII table in such a way that characters 0 to 31 are omitted and all the other characters are categorized and displayed in the table like this:

Special: 38 = '&'
Number: 48 = '0'
Letter: 68 = 'D'
and so on…

In previous projects I have used `if...then...else` blocks to test conditions and take alternative actions. Load up the *ifelse* project. You'll see that I have added an `if...then...else` to this new version of the ASCII table.

The way this works is that it does a number of complicated tests on the variable, `i`, to see if it falls between particular sets of values:

```
ifelse
if ((i >= 32) and (i <= 47)) or ((i >= 58) and (i <= 64))
   or ((i >= 91) and ((i <= 96)) or (i >= 123)) then
      s := 'Special : '
else if (i >= 48) and (i <= 57) then
      s := 'Number  : '
else if ((i >= 65) and (i <=90)) or ((i >= 97) and (i <=122)) then
      s := 'Letter  : ';
```

Consider the first test here (which I've reformatted so that it is easier to see the individual parts of the text arranged on new lines):

```
ifelse
if ((i >= 32) and (i <= 47))
   or ((i >= 58) and (i <= 64))
   or ((i >= 91) and ((i <= 96))
   or (i >= 123)) then
       s := 'Special : '
```

This could be translated into English as:

> '**if** *i is greater than or equal to 32 and i is also less than or equal to 47,*
> **or** *if i is greater than or equal to 58 and i is also less than or equal to 64,*
> **or** *if i is greater than or equal to 91 and i is also less than or equal to 96,*
> **or** *if i is greater than or equal to 123'*
> **then** *assign the string 'Special : ' to the variable, s."*

Boolean Tests

and and or are Boolean operators. In order to return true, the tests on both sides of and must be true; in order to return true, either one of the tests on either side of or must be true.

Example:

```
(true and true)       // returns true
(true and false)      // returns false
(true or true)        // returns true
(true or false)       // returns true
```

This long multi-condition test in the *ifelse* project works correctly but it is far from being elegant. Chaining together lots of tests linked by `and` and `or` can make the code difficult to understand. Worse still, in the *ifelse* project, the results of those complicated tests may cause other blocks the code following the `if` and `else` keywords to be run. And those bits of code contain yet more `and` and `or` tests. It is really hard to look at all this code and understand which tests will succeed for any specific character. Code that's hard to understand can often contain in hard-to-spot mistakes. Luckily, there is a much neater alternative to `if...then...else` when performing complex, multiple-choice tests. It's called a 'case' statement.

'case' Statements

Load up the *casetest* project and find the `FormCreate` procedure:

casetest

```
procedure TForm1.FormCreate(Sender: TObject);
var
    i : integer;
    s : string;
begin
    for i := 0 to 255 do
    begin
        s := '';
        case (i) of
            32..47,
            58..64,
            91..96,
            123..255: s := 'Special : ';
            48..57: s := 'Number  : ';
            65..90, 97..122:  s := 'Letter  : ';
        end;
        if s <> '' then
            ListBox1.Items.Add(Format('%s %d = ''%s''', [s, i, Chr(i)]));
   end;
end;
```

The code in this procedure has no longer has all those complicated `if` and `else` test conditions. In their place are some simple lists of numbers like this:

```
32..47,
58..64,
91..96,
123..255: s := 'Special : ';
```

This code here can be translated as:

> *"If a value falls between any of these ranges – 32 to 47, 58 to 64, 91 to 96, 123 to 255 – then assign the string 'Special : ' to the variable, s."*

Clearly even the English language 'translation' of this `case` test is much easier to understand than the `if` test I used previously with all its `and` and `or` conditions. The only question that remains to be answered is which value am I testing here?

It turns out that, as in the previous code, I am still testing the variable `i`. Only this time I don't need to include the variable in each individual part of the test as in:

```
if ((i >= 32) and (i <= 47)) or ((i >= 58)     // etc.
```

Instead, a whole block of tests is enclosed between the keywords `case` and `end`. A `case` statement such as this specifies the variable to be tested just once at the top of the block:

```
case (i) of
```

The variable must be of a simple ordinal type (a type with sequential values) such as `integer` or `char`. You cannot use string variables. The parentheses around the variable are optional in Pascal, but they are obligatory in many other languages. Following this so-called 'case selector' comes a list of possible values for the variable being tested. You can test one value at a time, if you like:

```
32: s := 'Space';
```

Or you can specify a sequential range of values separated by two dots:

```
48..57: s := 'Number  : ';
```

Ranges

Two dots .. are 'range markers'. They indicate a series of values starting with the value on the left of the dots and ending with the value on the right. If you want to have multiple, non-sequential ranges, these must be separated by commas like this:

```
1..2, 20..30, 101..205
```

Following each test, you must place a colon. Then comes the code to be executed which can either be a single line terminated by a semicolon or it may be a number of lines between the `begin` and `end` keywords. Optionally, a `case` statement can specify an `else` clause which will be executed if none of the preceding conditions is executed. The `TForm1.Button1Click` procedure in the *casetest* project includes an `else` clause which has the effect of simplifying the code by eliminating the multiple ranges previously used to indicate the ASCII values for special characters:

casetest

```
case (i) of
    48..57: s := 'Number  : ';
    65..90, 97..122: s := 'Letter  : ';
    else s := 'Special : ';
end;
```

Here is another example of a `case` statement, this time testing a `char` variable instead of an integer:

```
procedure TForm1.Button1Click(Sender: TObject);
var
  ch : char;
  s  : string;
begin
    ch := Chr(65);
    case(ch) of
       'a'..'z' : s := 'LowerCase';
       'A'..'Z' : begin
                    s := 'UpperCase';
                    Caption := ch;
                 end;
       else s := 'Not a letter';
   end;
     ShowMessage(s);
end;
```

'while' and 'repeat' Loops

In all the projects so far, we have iterated through a fixed series of values, 0 to 255, using a `for` loop. This is all very well just so long as you know what the ending value will be before you start running the loop. However, there are many occasions when you won't know what the end condition will be until the loop has already started running.

For instance, a program that downloads a file from the Internet might not know how long that file is – that is, how much data it contains – until it gets to the end of the file. So it wouldn't make any sense to say something like:

```
for i := 1 to 100 do
    readlines(i);
```

After all the file might contain 101 lines, 1,001 lines or no lines at all. It would make more sense to say:

```
while (morelines) do
    readlines();
```

Or you might say:

```
repeat
    readlines();
until (nomorelines);
```

Object Pascal provides `while` and `repeat` loops for just this sort of task. The principal difference between these two loops is that the test condition comes at the *end* of a `repeat` loop but at the *beginning* of a `while` loop. This means that a `repeat` loop always executes at least once whereas a `while` loop may never execute at all if its condition evaluates to false the first time it is tested.

In most cases it is purely a matter of personal preference whether you use a `while` or a `repeat` loop. Indeed, it may be better to standardize on one of them. To see these loops (*for*, *while* and *repeat*) in action, load up the *loops* project. This uses all three loops to copy some lines of text from a memo into a list box.

'for' Loop

Using a `for` loop, I count through the lines in `Memo1` (from the first at line 0 to the last which is given by the `Count` of lines less 1) and I add each line to `ListBox1`:

loops

```
for i := 0 to Memo1.Lines.Count - 1 do
    ListBox1.Items.Add(Memo1.Lines[i]);
```

Zero-based lists

Often arrays or lists of items start with index 0. The index of the final item will always be one less than the total number of items in that list. That's why you need to subtract 1 to find the index of the final item.

'repeat' Loop

Using a `repeat` loop, I first test that `Memo1` is not empty (so its `Count` is not 0) and, if it isn't empty, I find the line at index `i` in `Memo1`, add it to `ListBox1`, then add 1 to `i` and carry on doing this until `i` is equal to the number or `Count` of lines in `Memo1` at which point the loop stops running:

```
i := 0;
if not(Memo1.Lines.Count = 0) then
repeat
    ListBox1.Items.Add(Memo1.Lines[i]);
    i := i + 1;
until i = Memo1.Lines.Count;
```

'while' Loop

Using a `while` loop, I test that the `Count` of lines in `Memo1` is greater than `i`. The code in the loop runs while this test is true. At each turn through the loop, I add the line at index `i` in `Memo1` to `ListBox1`, then I add 1 to `i`. Eventually the `Count` of lines will no longer be greater than the value of `i`, at which point the loop stops running:

```
i := 0;
while (Memo1.Lines.Count > i) do
begin
    ListBox1.Items.Add(Memo1.Lines[i]);
    i := i + 1;
end
```

So which of these loops would be the best choice here? Since I know the number of lines in `Memo1` from the outset (it is returned by the `Memo1.Lines.Count` property, a `for` loop would be the simplest technique to use. A `for` loop is a good choice for iterating over a collection of a fixed length when that length can be easily calculated. In cases where the number of lines is unknown at the outset, a `repeat` or `while` loop would be a better choice.

When you've understood this code, load up the *washer* project. This uses the three types of loops to control the wash and spin cycles of a virtual computerized washing machine. It displays an animated circle to show that the machine is running a wash cycle. In order to make this circle vibrate at a visible frequency, I have had to write a `Delay` procedure which takes a parameter, `num`, and creates a delay by counting through `num` milliseconds:

washer

```
procedure Delay(num: integer);
var
    tc :longint;
begin
    tc :=GetTickCount;
    repeat
        Application.ProcessMessages;
    until ((GetTickCount-tc) >= num);
end;
```

GetTickCount

`GetTickCount` retrieves the number of milliseconds that have elapsed. My code assigns a start time to the variable `tc` then keeps subtracting the start time from the current time returned by `GetTickCount`. When that is greater than or equal to (`>=`) the value of `num`, then `num` milliseconds have elapsed:

```
procedure Delay(num: integer);
var
    tc: longint;
begin
    tc := GetTickCount;
    repeat
        Application.ProcessMessages;
    until ((GetTickCount - tc) >= num);
end;
```

At that point the `repeat` loop condition evaluates to `true` and the loop stops running. Note the code line inside the loop:

```
Application.ProcessMessages;
```

This instructs my program to process any events that need to be handled while the loop runs. Without this, the `repeat` loop itself would hog all the processor time and other events (such as my simple animation in this program) would not be dealt with.

The Windows unit in Lazarus

If you are using the Lazarus IDE rather than Delphi, you must be sure to add either `Windows` or `LclIntf` to the `uses` section of your code in order to have access to `GetTickCount`. The `Windows` unit provides routines specific to the Windows platform. the `LclIntf` unit provides routines for cross-platform development.

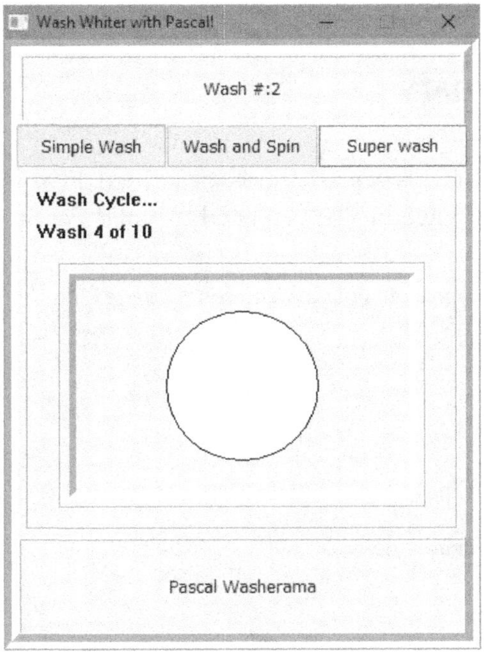

The virtual washing machine which proves that Pascal washes whiter!

You need to take care when using `while` and `repeat` loops to ensure that a valid end condition inevitably occurs at some stage. Look at the code below. This `repeat` loop continues executing until the function `Clean(clothes)` returns `true`. It does this when the value of the `clothes` variable equals 2. There is a bug in the code. See if you can find it:

```
{ This code contains a bug! }
clothes := 0;
repeat
    DisplayPanel.Caption := 'Wash #:' + IntToStr(clothes);
    WashCycle(100, 10);
until Clean(clothes);
```

The problem here is that the value of `clothes` will *never* equal 2. It will always remain at its original value, 0. That means that the loop will run indefinitely. You can find the fixed version of this code in the `SuperwashBtnClick` procedure:

```
clothes := 0;
repeat
    clothes := clothes + 1;    { this ensures a valid end condition }
    DisplayPanel.Caption := 'Wash #:' + IntToStr(clothes);
    WashCycle(100, 10);
until Clean(clothes);
```

Loops: Syntax Summary

This is the syntax of the three types of loops described in this chapter were the text between angle brackets would need to be replaced by valid Pascal code:

```
for <integer variable> := <start value> to <end value> do
begin
    <code to be repeated>
end;

repeat
    <code to be repeated>
until <this condition is true>

while <this condition is true> do
begin
    <code to be repeated>
end;
```

Arrays

Take a look at the *ascii2* project. This is an ASCII table which displays descriptions of some non-printing characters such 'TAB' for ASCII 8 and 'CARRIAGE RETURN' for ASCII 13. It does this by examining the items in two fixed-size lists or 'arrays'. The first array, `numarray`, contains numbers representing selected ASCII values. The second array, `strarray`, contains the string descriptions of those same characters:

```
numarray: array [1 .. 7] of integer = (0, 8, 9, 10, 13, 27, 32);
strarray: array [1 .. 7] of string = ('NULL', 'BACKSPACE', 'TAB',
                  'LINEFEED', 'CARRIAGE RETURN', 'ESCAPE', 'SPACE');
```

A `repeat` loop iterates through all the items in `numarray`, looking for a number that matches the current value, `asciivalue`. If a match is found at the current position, given by the index `i` in `numarray`, the code assigns the string found at index `i` in `strarray` to the string variable `s`:

ascii2

```
if numarray[i] = index then
    s := strarray[i];
```

Arrays provides a useful means of storing numerous items of data in a single structure and they are often used in conjunction with loops.

Let's look at some other examples of arrays. Load up the *arrays* project. Double-click the first button, labelled '*Array of Strings*'. This declares and initializes the variable, `sarray`, which is an array of four strings. These strings are displayed in a `Memo` when the button is clicked:

arrays

```
var
    sarray : array[1..4] of string;
begin
    sarray[1] := 'One';
    sarray[2] := 'Two';
    sarray[3] := 'Three';
    sarray[4] := 'Four';
end;
```

The code above declares an array of four 'slots' (the range `[1..4]`) capable of holding string items. To access a given 'slot' I use array notation by placing an index in square brackets, so this is how I put the string 'Two' into slot number 2:

```
sarray[2] := 'Two';
```

Array Ranges

Arrays may hold data items of almost any type as long as the array is declared to be `of` the appropriate type. Arrays have a fixed length. If you have an array indexed `1..4`, you cannot access an item at index 0 or 5. If you attempt to do so, you will generate an 'out of range' error.

The Array Start Index

Pascal allows you to specify the start index of an array. In the example shown earlier, that index is 1:

```
sarray : array[1..4] of string;
```

In many languages arrays are indexed from 0 by default. If you wish to index from 0 in Pascal, you can do so. The code shown below uses a 0-based array:

```
var
    sarray : array[0..3] of string;
begin
    sarray[0] := 'One';
    sarray[1] := 'Two';
    sarray[2] := 'Three';
    sarray[3] := 'Four';
end;
```

With zero-based arrays, bear in mind that the uppermost index is determined by the *length of the array -1*. The `Length` function can be used to return the length of an array. With the zero-based array shown above, this is how I would display the last string, 'Four', in the caption of my form:

```
Caption := sarray[Length(sarray)-1];
```

In the *arrays* project, I add each string item to the array one at a time. You might think it would be useful to be able to declare and assign all the items in an array all in one step. In Pascal, the way to do this is to declare an array as a constant. To do this, you precede its declaration with the word `const` rather than `var`. At the end of the declaration you can then place a simple equals sign, `=`, (not the usual `:=` assignment operator!) followed by a comma-separated list of values between parentheses. You can see an example of this type of array assignment in the procedure `TForm1.ConstStrArrayBtnClick` which initialises the slots of the array, `InitArray`, with the four strings shown in brackets:

```
const
    InitArray : Array[1..4] of string = ('Un', 'Deux', 'Trois', 'Quatre');
```

In spite of being declared as a `const`, the individual items in an array initialized in this way *can* be changed.

Notice that my `for` loop here uses the functions `Low` and `High` to return the first and last index of the array. These functions are useful in cases when the same piece of code may need to iterate through several different arrays each of which may have a different size:

```
for i := Low(InitArray) to High(InitArray) do
    Memo2.Lines.Add(InitArray[i]);
```

Now look at the event-handler for the button labelled, *'One Line Altered Case'*. This button takes the first line from `Memo1`, changes the case of each letter and then displays the result in `Memo2`. The fourth button does the same thing for all the lines in `Memo1`. They do this by calling the `ChangeCase` function which I have written higher up in the unit:

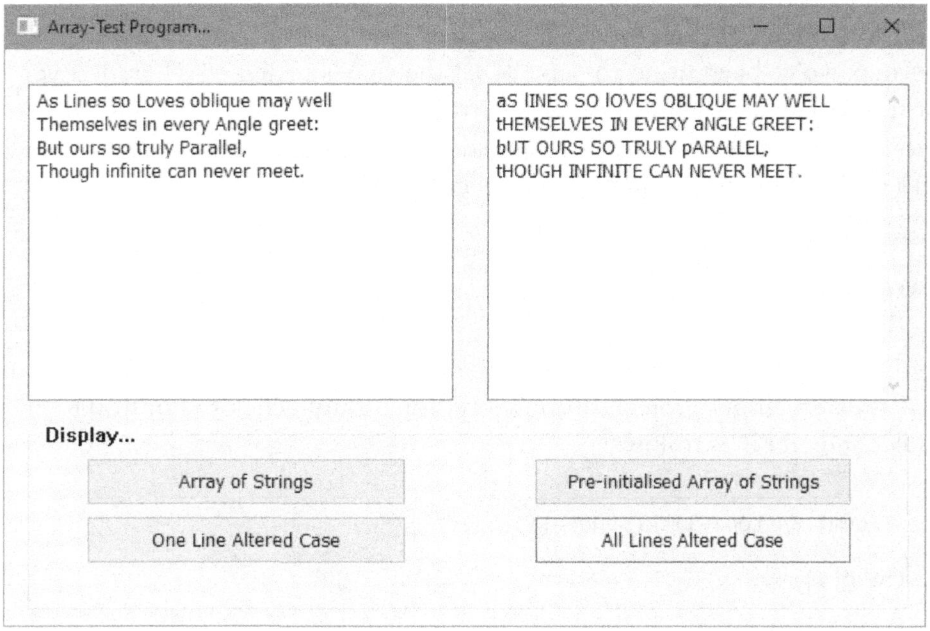

LowCase

I've written my own `LowCase` function to complement Delphi's `UpCase` function. In fact, Delphi also provides some other case-changing functions such as `AnsiUpperCase` and `AnsiLowerCase`.

The `ChangeCase` function iterates through the characters in the string from character 1 to the final character (returned by the `Length` function):

```
for i := 1 to Length(s)
```

If the character falls within the range of values between lowercase 'a' and a lowercase 'z' (as defined by the ASCII table), then it sets the character to uppercase using the standard `UpCase` function. Otherwise, it sets it to lowercase using my `LowCase` function:

```
for i := 1 to Length(s) do
    if (s[i] >= 'a') and (s[i] <= 'z') then
        s[i] := UpCase(s[i])
    else
        s[i] := LowCase(s[i]);
```

This code counts through the string using an integer variable `i` between square brackets to get or set a character at each index. The syntax used should look familiar. It is exactly the same syntax we've been using to get and set the values in arrays. There is a very good reason for this. A Pascal string is, in fact, an array of characters.

In traditional Pascal it used to be required that all strings were defined with a fixed array length declared between square brackets in this manner:

```
var
    s : string[10];
```

Fixed-length string declarations are still an option in Delphi. For example, try the following. Create an empty project, drop in a button, double-click the button to create an event-handler and edit it as follows:

```
procedure TForm1.Button1Click(Sender: TObject);
var
    s : string[4];
begin
    s := 'Hello world';
    Caption := s;
end;
```

Run the application and notice the form's caption when you click the button:

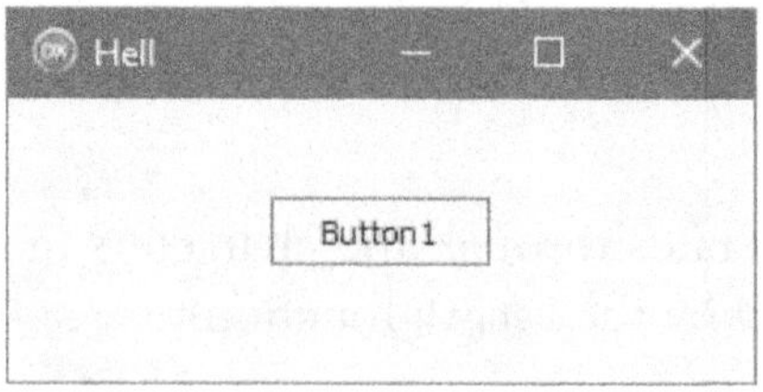

From this you can deduce how Object Pascal deals with a string array overrun – that is, when you try to add more elements to an array than the array can contain. When you attempt to put more characters into the string than there are slots available (here there are 11 characters but only 4 slots) the string is truncated. Other programming languages may not do this. In C, for example, it is perfectly possible to overwrite bits of memory by trying to fit more data into a string than will actually fit. This can easily crash a program. It is a good idea, therefore, to get into the habit of checking that you stick within the declared range of a string or an array.

Unicode Strings

The default `string` type in modern versions of Delphi is a `UnicodeString` which may whose maximum length is limited only by available memory. Delphi automatically handles memory allocation for this sort of string.

Arrays in Delphi

You will discover that arrays or array-like objects pop up all over the place in Delphi. For example, the `Lines` property of a `Memo` object can be indexed using array syntax. Notice that the first line in a `Memo` has the index 0 rather than 1 (see the section earlier in this chapter on *The Array Start Index*), so in the *arrays* project, you will see that I obtain the first line of *Memo1* in this way:

```
s := Memo1.Lines[0];
```

In the *ascii2* project, when I used the `Format` function to add a string to `ListBox1, I` placed variables such as `i` and `charname`, separated by commas between square brackets. This again looks like an array:

```
ListBox1.Items.Add(Format('%d = ''%s''', [i, charname]));
```

This is how the Delphi help system documents the `Format` function:

```
function Format(const Format: string; const Args: array of const): string;
```

So here the first argument passed to the `Format` function is a string and the second is, indeed, an array. An '`array of const`' is rather a special type of array since it can be 'open' (that is, it can be of variable length) and it can contain mixed types of data. In my code above, for instance, `i` is an integer and `charname` is a string. Most arrays do not allow mixed data types in this way but an `array of const` does.

Formatting Strings

The `Format` function provides a convenient alternative to using conversion routines, such as `IntToStr` to insert data into strings. Each item in the array is inserted into the string at the position of a marker such as `'%d'` indicating that a decimal (integer) argument is expected or `'%s'` indicating a string argument.

You may notice there are two examples of pre-initialized array-type constants in the *ascii2* project: `numarray` contains some ASCII values and `strarray` contains string descriptions of those values:

```
const
    numarray : array[1..7] of integer = (0,8,9,10,13,27,32);
    strarray : array[1..7] of string =
                          ('NULL','BACKSPACE','TAB','LINEFEED',
                           'CARRIAGE RETURN','ESCAPE','SPACE');
```

Typed Constants

It is also possible in Object Pascal to declare other varieties of pre-initialized constants called 'typed constants'. This is how to declare a typed constant. The names between angle-brackets would, in real code, be replaced by valid identifiers:

```
<SomeName> : <SomeType> = <SomeValue>;
```

Here are some examples:

```
const
    myStr : String = 'Hello world';
    myInt : integer = 10;
    myDbl : double = 2.5;
```

Typed Constants Aren't Constants!

Somewhat illogically, the values of typed 'constants' are variable. They can be assigned new values during the course of program execution. This is unlike the behaviour of most identifiers declared beneath the keyword `const` which cannot be changed in this way! See the Appendix for more information on typed constants.

True Constants

Even though you need to know about typed constants, I suggest that you avoid them in your own code. True constants are more generally useful than typed constants. For an example, look at the *arrays* project which declares two string constants at the head of the unit, `MY_CAPTION` and `MY_OTHER_CAPTION`:

```
const
    MY_CAPTION = 'Pascal is Great!';
    MY_OTHER_CAPTION = 'But I''d rather a case of Champagne!';
```

These two constants are used by the top two buttons on the form. When you click them the form's caption is set to one of the constants. Notice that you don't need to specify the type of `const` (such as `string` or `integer`) when it is defined. This is the syntax of a true constant:

```
<SomeName> = <SomeValue>;
```

Here are some examples:

```
const
    MSG = 'You cannot change this!';
    HUNDRED = 100;
    THOUSAND =  10 * HUNDRED;
    GAP = ' ';
```

Given the declarations above, you can now write code such as:

```
Caption := MSG + GAP + IntToStr(HUNDRED) + GAP + IntToStr(THOUSAND);
```

Once you have declared true constants, you cannot change their values later in your code. You might try to do so, say by inserting this line into your code:

```
MSG := 'A new message';
```

But the Pascal compiler would refuse to compile the program. Because the value assigned to a constant cannot be changed.

Local Constants

Constants can have differing 'scopes' just like variables. For instance, in the *washer* project the `TForm1.Clean` procedure declares this 'local' constant:

```
const
    REALLYCLEAN = 2;
```

The function `TForm1.Dry` procedure declares another local constant:

```
const
    REALLYDRY = 4;
```

Why Use Constants?

Constants are useful for two main reasons. First they help to clarify your code. The test `if (clothes < REALLYCLEAN)` is more descriptive than one that states `if (clothes < 2)`. Secondly, constants help to avoid repetition in your code. Let's suppose you were writing a banking program. If an investor's bank balance falls below -$100 you display the error message: *'You are in debt! Pay up at once!'*.

Now let's suppose this program contains 100 procedures, each of which contains code similar to the following:

```
if Balance <= -100 then
    ShowMessage('You are in debt! Pay up at once!');
```

But one day the bank decides that overdrafts will only applied when the balance falls below $150. Moreover, there have also been complaints from customers that the warning message is too abrupt.

You are told to rewrite the program to fix these matters. This means you will have to go through each of those 100 procedures altering *-100* to *-150* (you can't just do a search and replace since you might accidentally replace the value *-100* in some inappropriate procedure).

Then you will have to rewrite all the error messages too. You could have avoided all this trouble by declaring these constants at the top of the unit:

```
const
    MSG = 'You are in debt! Pay up at once!';
    INDEBT = -100;
```

Each of the procedures could now contain this code:

```
if Balance <= INDEBT then
    ShowMessage(MSG);
```

Now, when you receive the order to rewrite the messages displayed by your program, you only need to alter the values of the two constants:

```
const
    MSG = 'Oh dear, you seem to be having a cash-flow problem.';
    INDEBT = -150;
```

The code in each of your 100 procedures will now automatically use these new constant values. Just by declaring two constants we have made our program shorter to write, easier to understand and simpler to maintain.

Capital Letters For Constants?

I've written my constant names in capital letters. This is a common programing convention. It is not enforced, however, and many Pascal programmers use mixed-case identifiers for constants such as `InDebt` or insert underscores to separate the 'words' such as `IN_DEBT`. Personally, I like to use all upper-case (with or without underscores) as it makes it immediately obvious that the identifier is a constant rather than a variable.

Chapter 6 – User Defined Types and File IO

In this chapter we discover how to define your own custom data types and save your data into files on disk.

Let's suppose you want to create a database of your album collection. For the sake of simplicity, I'll assume this is a database of CDs but it could equally well be MP3s or DVDs or any other type of audio or video medium. In this hypothetical program, I could declare arrays of CD variables. These could represent the ten slots of a CD changer or the 100 slots of a CD storage rack:

```
var
    cdChanger : array[1..10] of CD;
    cdRack : array[1..100] of CD;
```

The only trouble with this is that, unlike `string` or `integer`, `CD` is not a known data type. This is not a major problem, however, because Pascal lets you create user-defined types. At its simplest, a user-defined type might be based on an existing type such as `string`. If, for example, I wanted my `CD` data type to contain the name of the CD as a string with a maximum length of 45 characters this is how I would declare it:

```
type
    CD = string[45];
```

Custom Data Types

Type declarations always begin with an identifier followed by an equals sign and the type-definition itself:

```
type
    <Identifier> = <Type Definition>;
```

Once a type has been declared you can create variables of that type. Assuming that I've already defined the `CD` type (a 45 character string) as shown earlier, this is how I declare a `CD` variable called `aCD` and a ten-slot `CD` array called `cdChanger`:

```
var
    aCD: CD;
    cdChanger : array[1..10] of CD;
```

In the *usertype* project I've declared a `CD` data type and a `cdChanger` array variable inside the `TForm1.Button3Click` procedure. A `for` loop counts through the array and displays the name of each `CD` in `Memo1`:

usertype

```
procedure TForm1.Button3Click(Sender: TObject);
type
    CD = string[45];
var
    cdChanger: array [1 .. 10] of CD;
    i: integer;
begin
    cdChanger[1] := 'Dolly Parton''s Great Hits';
    cdChanger[2] := 'Village People Sing Led Zeppelin';
    cdChanger[3] := 'The Wombles House-Mix';
    cdChanger[4] := 'Wagner''s Quiet Bits';
    cdChanger[5] := 'Pavarotti Sings ABBA';
    cdChanger[6] := 'George Michael In Neasden';
    cdChanger[7] := 'Judas Priest Great Love Songs';
    cdChanger[8] := 'The Andrews Sisters Lost Sessions';
    cdChanger[9] := 'Ken Dodd Sings Buddy Can You Spare A Buttie?';
    cdChanger[10] := 'Celine Dion''s Tribute To MeatLoaf';
    for i := 1 to 10 do
        Memo1.Lines.Add(cdChanger[i]);
end;
```

Displaying ' in a string

Note that I've put two `'` characters together in the string `'Dolly Parton''s Great Hits'`. Since the `'` character is used to delimit the start and end of a string, you cannot insert a single `'` into a string because that would mark the end of the string. You can, however, insert two `'` characters like this: `''`. When the string is displayed, only one `'` character will be shown.

So far, my program it isn't really all that useful. After all, the `CD` data type is just a string. I might just as well have declared `cdChanger` to be an array of `string`:

```
var
   CDChanger : array[1..10] of string;
```

The `CD` data type would be more useful if it were able to store more information than just the album title. In a real-world database, you would probably also want to store the name of the artist, the price of the disc and perhaps the record label too.

It turns out that it is perfectly possible to create new types that include multiple data-fields capable of storing all that information. I'll show how this is done later on. First, however, let's take a look at some other examples of user-defined types in the *usertype* project.

At the top of the *utunit.pas* unit, I have declared these types:

```
type
    Str10 = string[10];
    Str5  = string[5];
    DaysInWeek = (Mon,Tue,Wed,Thu,Fri,Sat,Sun);
    UpperCase = 'A'..'Z';
```

Order of declaration

The order in which the types are declared is significant. Here I have had to place my declaration of the `DaysInWeek` type above the declaration of `TForm1` (Delphi's automatically-added code defining the Form). If I had placed it below that declaration the program would not compile. That is because a parameter of the `DaysInWeek` type is used by the `DayStr` function of `TForm1`:

```
function DayStr(day: DaysInWeek): string;
```

The Delphi compiler works downwards from the top of the file and it needs to have found the type declaration above any parameters or variables which use that type.

My first two type declarations, `Str10` and `Str5`, are very simple. They define fixed-length strings with a maximum length of 10 and 5 characters respectively. The next declaration, `DaysInWeek`, is a bit more complicated. Instead of declaring a simple type, it declares a list of possible values from `Mon` to `Sun`. This is called an enumerated type.

Enumerated Types

An enumerated type defines a list of identifiers. It is called an enumerated type because it is possible to count or 'enumerate' the items in the list. The `DaysInWeek` type defines this list of identifiers: `Mon,Tue,Wed,Thu,Fri,Sat,Sun`:

```
DaysInWeek = (Mon,Tue,Wed,Thu,Fri,Sat,Sun);
```

Ranges

Finally, the `UpperCase` type specifies a range of values between capital 'A' and capital 'Z'. Recall from the previous chapter, that these values are sequential in the ASCII table:

```
UpperCase = 'A'..'Z';
```

In the `TForm1.Button1Click` procedure some variables have been declared using these data types:

```
var
    s10    : Str10;
    s5     : Str5;
    today  : DaysInWeek;
    letter : UpperCase;
```

Enumerated Type Identifiers

A constant called `GREETING` has been assigned the string 'Hello world'. Some code inside the procedure now assigns this constant to each of the two string variables:

```
s10 := GREETING;
s5 := GREETING;
```

The variable, `today`, is assigned the value `Wed`, which is one of the identifiers listed in the `DaysInWeek` enumerated type:

```
today := Wed;
```

Finally, the variable, `letter`, is assigned the uppercase char, 'X':

```
letter := 'X';
```

The `Format` function then creates a string to containing the values of these variables. It does this by copying the values from the second argument, an array between square brackets, into the first argument, a string, at locations marked with a `%` followed by a character such as `s` or `d`, where `%s` indicates a string and `%d` indicates a decimal (integer) value:

```
Format('s10 = %s, s5 = %s, today= %s, letter = %s',
      [s10, s5, DayStr(today), letter])
```

The formatted string is then passed to the `ShowMessage` procedure which displays it in a message box:

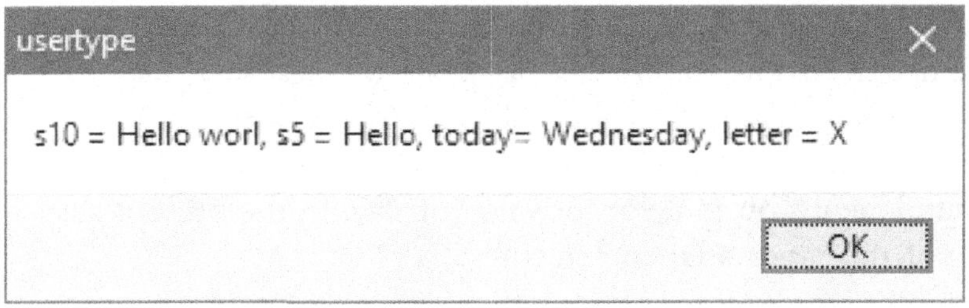

Pay close attention to the string that has been assigned to each of the two string variables. The first, `s10`, is a string of the type `Str10`. This can contain a maximum of 10 characters. The string constant, `GREETING`, has 11 characters. As a consequence, `str10` in effect loses the 11th character and therefore it displays 'Hello worl'. The second variable, `s5`, is a five-character string of the type `Str5` and it contains only the first five characters, 'Hello'. There are no surprises in the last variable, named `letter`. It was assigned the value 'X' in my code and that's just what's displayed in this dialog box.

Now consider the third variable, `today`. It is not possible to display the actual value of this variable, since the identifier which has been assigned to it, `Wed`, is not a string. If you look at the arguments which I passed to the `Format` function, you'll see that in order to obtain a string representation of this variable, I called the `DayStr` function with the `today` variable as an argument:

```
DayStr(today)
```

In my code, this function contains a `case` statement with a series of trigger values from `Mon` to `Sun`, corresponding to the values specified by the `DaysInWeek` enumerated type:

```
usertype
function TForm1.DayStr(day: DaysInWeek): string;
begin
    case(day) of
        Mon : result := 'Monday';
        Tue : result := 'Tuesday';
        Wed : result := 'Wednesday';
        Thu : result := 'Thursday';
        Fri : result := 'Friday';
        Sat : result := 'Saturday';
        Sun : result := 'Sunday';
        else result := 'Unknown';
    end;
end;
```

Here I am using `result` (a variable that is automatically pre-defined for functions and which has the same data type as the function declaration) to return a value from this function. As explained in Chapter 3, Object Pascal allows *either* the function name – here that is `DayStr` – *or* the variable `result` to be used to return a value.

The `DaysInWeek` parameter named `day` is used as the `case` selector here. The function returns a string that depends on the current value of `day`. In the present case, `day` equals `Wed`, so this branch of the `case` statement executes:

```
Wed : result := 'Wednesday';
```

As explained in the last chapter, the selector in a `case` statement must be an ordinal type. That is, it must be a type that has a fixed set of values which can be placed in order from the lowest to the highest. This is why integers and characters (whose order is fixed in the ASCII table) can be used as selectors but strings, which have no inherent order, cannot be used.

Order of Identifiers

Is there any intrinsic order in identifiers such as `Mon` or `Wed`? It turns out that there is. To understand this, turn to the code of `TForm1.Button2Click`. You'll see that this counts through the identifiers in the `DaysInWeek` enumerated type using a `for` loop:

```
for i := 0 to 6 do
    s := s + DayStr(DaysInWeek(i)) + ' ';
```

Each time the loop executes, the `DayStr` function is called with an identifier from the `DaysInWeek` type:

```
DaysInWeek = (Mon,Tue,Wed,Thu,Fri,Sat,Sun);
```

This identifier is determined by `for` loop's variable, `i`. So if `i` is 0 the first identifier, `Mon`, is selected; if `i` is 6 the last identifier (that is, the 7th), `Sun`, is selected. In the `DayStr` function, one of those `DaysInWeek` values (from `Mon` to `Sun`) is received as the `day` parameter, this matches a trigger in a `case` statement and a string is returned as a result.

This is how the string `s` is displayed in a message box:

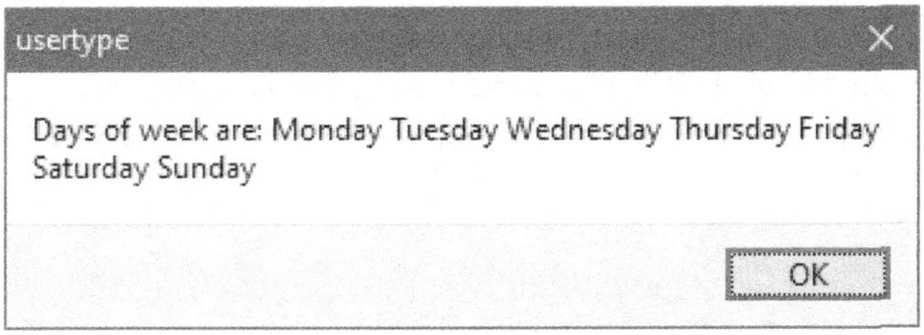

One of the advantages of declaring enumerated types such as this is that they can add to the clarity of your code. A test such as `if day = Wed` is easier to read and understand than `if day = 2`.

Type Checking

The other advantage of enumerated types is that, when you declare a type, the compiler will check that variables of that type fall within a meaningful range. For example, if `day` is a variable of type `DaysInWeek`, the compiler will refuse to compile code that assigns or tests values that are not within the bounds of that type. The following test, for example, would not compile:

```
if day = Fun
```

For another example of the compiler's type-checking, find the assignment to the variable, `letter`, in the `TForm1.Button1Click` procedure:

```
letter := 'X';
```

Change this assignment from an uppercase 'X' to a lowercase 'x' and try to run the program. The compilation will fail and you should see an error message similar to the following:

```
[dcc32 Error] utunit.pas(65): E1012 Constant expression violates subrange bounds
```

To understand the compiler's error message, look back at the declaration of the `UpperCase` data type:

```
UpperCase = 'A'..'Z';
```

This specifically limits the characters that can be assigned to an `UpperChar` variable to uppercase letters between 'A' and 'Z'. The Pascal compiler is quite strict in its type-checking. This lets you fix potential errors that would otherwise result in bugs.

Records

Now let's return to the problem of creating a more complex data type with multiple fields such as the name, artist and price of each CD in our collection. In Pascal, one way of doing this is by defining a 'record' type. This is the syntax of a record declaration:

```
type
<TypeIdentifier> = record
    <FieldIdentifier> : <Type>;
    <[Optionally more fields]>
end;
```

In real code, the items shown between angle-brackets would be replaced by appropriate identifiers and types. An example can be found in the *cdrecs* project. Towards the top of the unit you will see the following record type has been defined:

cdrecs

```
CD = record
    name    : Str30;
    artist  : Str30;
    price   : double;
    cdlabel : Str30;
end;
```

The `CD` record type contains three fields of the user-defined type, `Str30`, which has previously been declared to be a string of 30 chars (`string[30]`). The `price` field is a floating-point variable of the type `double`. Before you can use a `CD` record, you need to create a variable of the `CD` type. This is done in the `var` section at the top of the code unit:

```
aCD   : CD;
```

The fields of the `aCD` record are assigned values in the `TForm1.FormCreate` procedure which executes when the program is run:

```
aCD.name := 'Loads of Nice Tunes';
aCD.artist := 'Blaise & The Pascalettes';
aCD.price := 0.75;
aCD.CDlabel := 'Seedy CDs';
```

Notice how dot-notation is used to refer to the fields of a record, where the dot is put after the variable name and before the field name. However, unless you have a very tiny CD collection, one record all on its own isn't going to be very useful. What we need is a structure capable of storing a list of records. The obvious candidate is an array. In the unit's `var` section, you will see that I have declared this four-slot array:

```
myCDs : array[1..4] of CD;
```

This array is filled with four `CD` records in `TForm1.FormCreate` by specifying each array index followed by one of the four fields and an assignment statement. Once again, notice how I have used dot-notation. This code that initializes a single `CD` record in the first slot of the `myCDs` array:

```
myCDs[1].name := 'Great Hits';
myCDs[1].artist := 'Dolly Parton';
myCDs[1].price := 10.75;
myCDs[1].CDlabel := 'Stony Records';
```

Now, whenever I want to examine the data of a particular CD, I can just refer to the record at a given index in the array. The `TForm1.ShowCD` procedure takes an integer argument, `i`, which is used to index the array. This is how it retrieves the value of the `name` field from the record at index `i`:

```
myCDs[i].name
```

In fact, my code uses dot-notation to retrieve all the field values of a `CD` record at index `i` and it displays these values in a formatted string (as explained in Chapter 5):

```
Memo1.Lines.Add
    (Format('CDRec[%d] is %s by %s, on the %s label. Price = $%n.',
     [i, myCDs[i].name, myCDs[i].artist, myCDs[i].cdlabel, myCDs[i].price]));
```

The `TForm1.ShowCDsBtnClick` procedure uses a `for` loop to increment the value of `i` from 1 to 4. Calling `ShowCD(i)` from inside this loop has the effect of displaying the data of all the records from index 1 to 4 of the array:

```
for i := 1 to 4 do
    ShowCD(i);
```

The user also has the option of entering a specific number into the `Edit1` text field. When the `TForm1.FindCDBtnClick` procedure executes, this attempts to convert the contents of `Edit1` (the `Text` property which is a string) into an integer and to display the data from the record at that index. This is a simplified version of the procedure:

```
i := StrToInt(Edit1.Text);
ShowCD(i);
```

Error Handling

In fact, if you load up my code from the source code archive you will see that the `FindCDBtnClick` procedure contains far more code than is shown in the simplified version above. This is due to the fact that I have had to do quite a bit of error-checking. For instance, I check that the value of `i` is a valid index into the array. Since the slots are numbered 1 to 4, I have tested that `i` is greater than 0 and less than 5:

```
if (i > 0) and (i < 5)
```

I have also had to handle another potentially disastrous error. There is nothing to prevent the user entering a string such as 'Hello' which cannot possibly be converted into an integer. When a program attempts to perform an impossible task of this sort, it generates an error called an 'exception'.

In Delphi, a data-conversion error is an exception of the type `EConvertError`. My program attempts to trap any such error and recover from it without crashing. We'll look at exception-handling in more detail in Chapter 9. This is the full code listing of the `FindCDBtnClick` procedure, including error-handling:

cdrecs

```
procedure TForm1.FindCDBtnClick(Sender: TObject);
var
    ok: boolean;
    i: integer;
begin
    Memo1.Clear;
    ok := true;
    try
        i := StrToInt(Edit1.Text);
    except
        on e: EConvertError do
        begin
            ShowMessage('You must enter a number!');
            ok := false;
        end;
    end;
    if ok then
        if (i > 0) and (i < 5) then
            ShowCD(i)
        else
            ShowMessage('Enter a number between 1 and 4!');
end;
```

IO – Input/Output

My CD database suffers from one enormous limitation: the records are 'hard-coded' into the application itself so, if I wanted to add new records or modify existing ones, I would need to rewrite the code and recompile the program.

It would be far more useful to be able to modify the data from within the application and save any changes into a file on disk. Then, when the program is next run, that data could be reloaded.

In order to be able to do this we need to learn how to handle disk files and I/O (Input/Output). I do that in the *cddbase* project. This includes a ready-made sample data file, '*MyCDs.dat*' which is loaded when the program runs.

A Gentle Warning

At first sight, File IO (writing and reading data) may seem enormously complicated. While I've tried to keep things simple in this chapter, you may nevertheless find that it takes some thinking about in order to work out exactly what is going on. *Don't panic!* Take time to try out my sample programs and examine the code carefully. You will soon discover that the essential routines are quite simple. However, you may need to add quite a bit of error-checking to make sure that you can deal with unexpected problems such as incorrect data being loaded by a program.

Before going any further, let's see what this program does. Run it. Leave the number at the bottom-right of the form at 0 and click the '*Load Record Number*' button. This should load and display details of a CD called 'Banjo Jamboree' by 'Bert's Big Bad Banjo Band':

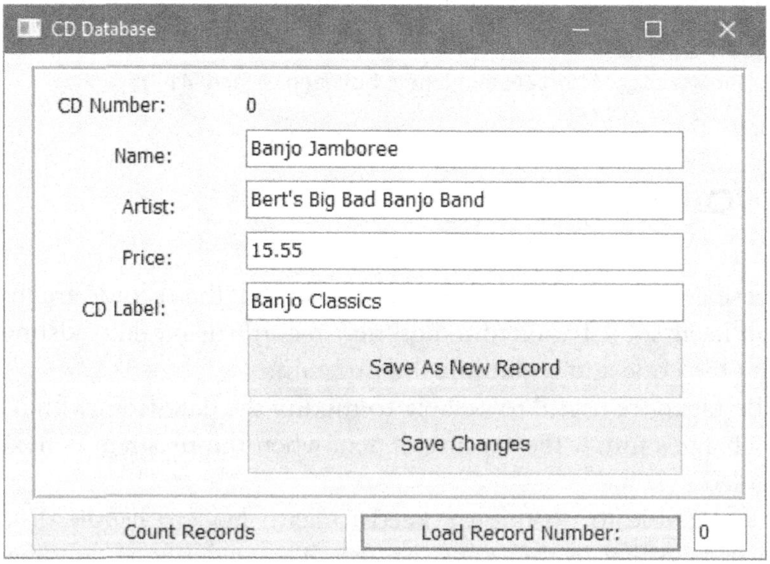

Change the number to 1 and click the button again to load up the next record from the data file. Try entering the number 50 in the edit box at the bottom right. Click '*Load Record Number*'. This time when you click the button you will be told that record 50 cannot be found.

Try creating a new record. Edit the first two fields so that they contain a different name and artist. Then click the '*Save As New Record*' button. This will add a new record to the end of the data file.

You can also modify an existing record. Enter 1 into the small edit field and click the button to load that record. Currently, this displays details of a CD called 'Whistling Hits' by Whistling Jack Ramsbottom. Change the name to 'Whistling Hits Volume 2'. Then click the button labelled '*Save Changes*'. The modified record will be saved back into the data file.

File Handling

This is the code listing of the `SaveCDRec` procedure which saves a record to a file on disk. You may want to refer back to this when reading the explanation that follows:

cddbase

```
procedure TForm1.SaveCDRec(saveAsNew: boolean);
var
    aCD: CD;
begin
    if FieldsOK then
    begin
        AssignFile(recFile, REC_FILE_NAME);
        if not FileExists(REC_FILE_NAME) then
            Rewrite(recFile) { Create a new file }
        else
            Reset(recFile);
        begin
            aCD.name := NameEd.Text;
            aCD.artist := ArtistEd.Text;
            aCD.price := StrToFloat(PriceEd.Text);
            aCD.cdlabel := CDLabelEd.Text;
            if saveAsNew then
            begin // --- create a new record
                Seek(recFile, FileSize(recFile));
                recPos := FilePos(recFile);
                FilePosLabel.Caption := IntToStr(recPos);
            end
            else // --- modify the record being edited
                Seek(recFile, recPos);
            Write(recFile, aCD);
            CloseFile(recFile);
        end;
    end;
end;
```

Let's see how the `CD` record-saving routine this has been programmed. If the program is still running, stop it. In the form-designer, double-click the '*Save As New Record*' button. This takes you into the editor where you will see that the button's event-handler this contains this single line:

cddbase

```
SaveCDRec(true);
```

The code attached to the '*Save Changes*' button in the `SaveChangesBtnClick` procedure is identical apart from the value of the Boolean argument:

```
SaveCDrec(false);
```

We'll find out what the Boolean argument does in a moment. Scroll up to find the procedure `TForm1.SaveCDRec`. This is where all the real work is done. First of all this procedure calls the `FieldsOK` function, which you'll find higher up in the unit. The `FieldsOK` function may look complicated at first sight but it really isn't. All it does is check that the data entered by the user is correct. If so, the remainder of the code in the `SaveCDRec` procedure is executed. We now arrive at this crucial line of code:

```
AssignFile(recFile, REC_FILE_NAME);
```

`AssignFile` is a Delphi procedure which associates the name of an external file with a file variable. Here `recFile` is my file variable. It is declared near the top of the unit:

```
recFile: File of CD;
```

`REC_FILE_NAME` is the name of the disk file itself. It is declared in the `const` section:

```
const
   REC_FILE_NAME = 'MyCDs.dat';
```

I shall use the file variable `recFile` when manipulating the file itself. First of all, my code uses the standard function, `FileExists` to check if the file, *'MyCDs.dat'*, exists. If it does not exist, then the code (in the `SaveCDRec` procedure) executes the `Rewrite` procedure:

```
if not FileExists(REC_FILE_NAME) then
   Rewrite(recFile)
```

Cross-platform file handling

In the cross-platform Lazarus IDE, the `FileExitsUTF8` function is recommended in preference to `FileExists`. This is because the `FileExistsUTF8` function handles different conventions for file and directory naming on different operating systems.

The `Rewrite` procedure both creates and opens a file. A file must be opened before you can save any data into it. If the file already exists, you don't need to create it but you do need to open it. The `Reset` procedure opens an existing file. This is the code that executes if *'MyCDs.dat'* does exist:

```
else
    Reset(recFile);
```

There now follows some code that initializes the fields of a new `CD` record, using data from the edit fields on the form:

```
aCD.name := NameEd.Text;
aCD.artist := ArtistEd.Text;
aCD.price := StrToFloat(PriceEd.Text);
aCD.cdlabel := CDLabelEd.Text;
```

Saving Fixed Length Strings

The definition of the `CD` record type in the *cddbase* project is the same as the definition in the *cdrecs* project that we looked at earlier:

```
type
    Str30 = string[30];

CD = record
    name    : Str30;
    artist  : Str30;
    price   : double;
    cdlabel : Str30;
end;
```

If you intend to save records to disk, be sure that any string fields are fixed-length strings. Here, for example, three of the fields use the 30-character string type, `Str30`. This is because an ordinary string (without a length specified) is 'dynamically allocated'. The length of such a string is undefined. In principle a dynamically allocated string may have any length within the limits of your computer's memory. It is generally simpler and safer to use fixed-length strings when saving data to disk.

Next my code tests the value of the Boolean parameter, `saveAsNew`. Recall that this value is passed as `true` by the `SaveAsNewBtnClick` procedure and it is passed as `false` by `SaveChangesBtnClick`. If it is `true`, then the user wants to create a new record and save it at the end of the data file. This is the code that executes:

```
Seek(recFile,FileSize(recFile));
recPos := FilePos(recFile);
FilePosLabel.Caption := IntToStr(recPos);
```

FileSize in Lazarus

There are two versions of the `FileSize` function in Lazarus. One (in the `FileUtil` unit) takes a string argument – the file name; the other (in the `System` unit) takes a `File` variable. In Delphi, `FileSize` defaults to a `File` variable. To ensure that this is the version of `FileSize` that you use in Lazarus write `System.FileSize` when you call the function in your code, like this:

```
Seek(recFile,System.FileSize(recFile));
```

Random Access Files

The `Seek` procedure is used to find the record at a specific position in the file. In a 'random access' file which contains items of a specific data-type (such as a file of `CD` records), the `FileSize` function returns the number of items in the file.

A random access file is one whose contents are so structured that a particular chunk of data (here representing a 'record') can be accessed by specifying its location within the file. This contrasts with a sequential access file in which data is accessed by moving through the file from the beginning to the end in strict sequence. Look at this line of code:

```
Seek(recFile,FileSize(recFile));
```

This finds the position of the last record in the file and makes this the currently 'active' record position – that is, the position at which any operations on the file, such as accessing or modifying data, may be done. Another function, `FilePos`, may be used to identify the currently active record position in the file. This is how I assign the current record number to the global variable, `recPos`:

```
recPos := FilePos(recFile);
```

This allows me to display the record number in a label:

```
FilePosLabel.Caption := IntToStr(recPos);
```

If, on the other hand, the user clicks the '*Save Changes*' button, the program doesn't need to create a new record. Instead, it needs to save any modifications back into the record being edited at its original position in the data file. So, rather than seeking to the end of the file, we need to seek to the position of the current record number. Recall that the program stores the current record number in the `recPos` variable. So this line of code seeks to the current record:

```
Seek(recFile, recPos);
```

Having found the correct position in the data file, we now need to write the data:

```
Write(recFile, aCD);
```

Finally, having written the data, we must close the file:

```
CloseFile(recFile);
```

File IO Summary

At first sight all these file-handling routines this may seem confusing. So let's simplify it to its bare essentials. Here are the essential procedures needed to open an existing typed file, such as a file of records, and write a record into it:

```
AssignFile(<File variable>, <File Name>);
Reset(<File variable>);
Seek(<File variable>, <Position in File>);
Write(<File variable>, <Record>);
CloseFile(<File variable>);
```

In real code, the elements shown in angle-brackets are replaced by actual identifiers like this:

```
AssignFile(recFile, REC_FILE_NAME);
Reset(recFile);
Seek(recFile, FileSize(recFile));
Write(recFile, aCD);
CloseFile(recFile);
```

If you want to create a new file, use `Rewrite` rather than `Reset`. Loading data from a file is accomplished in a similar manner. The two main differences are that you must always use `Reset` and never use `Rewrite` and you must use `Read` instead of `Write`.

The code in the `TForm1.LoadBtnClick` procedure attempts to read in the record number, `recNum`, specified by the user. There is quite a lot of error checking in this code. While this checking is necessary, it may obscure the essential file-handling routines. Here, for clarity, is a simplified version:

```
AssignFile(RecFile, REC_FILE_NAME);
Reset(recFile);
Seek(recFile, recNum);
Read(recFile, aRecord);
CloseFile(recFile);
```

Notice that the `Read` procedure must be instructed to read the same data type (here `aRecord` has been declared to be of the `CD` type) as was previously written into the file by the `Write` procedure. Just as `Write` will write one record's worth of the specified data type to a file, `Read` will read back one record's worth of the specified data type.

Text Files

The other sort of file to which you may need to use from time to time is a plain text file. Unlike a random access file, a text file does not contain items of fixed types, such as records. It just contains characters. This means that you cannot use `Seek` to find an item at a specified position. Text files have to be processed sequentially. In other words, when you want to read or write data, you have to start at the top of the file and work through its contents one character or line of text at a time.

In spite of this fundamental difference, many of the routines needed to read and write text files are identical to those used with random access files. Once again, a file is opened using the `AssignFile` and `Reset` procedures prior to reading data; a file is opened with the `AssignFile` and `Rewrite` procedures prior to writing data. When you've finished with it, the file is closed using `CloseFile`.

Data can be read one character at a time using the `Read` procedure and written one character at a time using the `Write` procedure. Two additional reading and writing procedures are also available. `Readln` reads a whole line at a time (up to the Carriage-Return/Linefeed characters at the end of a line) and `Writeln` writes a new line into a file.

Of course, you have to make sure you don't try to read beyond the end of a text file. The `Eof` function helps out here. It returns `true` at the end of a file, `false` otherwise. Load up the *textread* project. In the form-designer, double-click the button labelled '*FileReadlnBtn*' to view the `FileReadlnBtnClick` procedure.

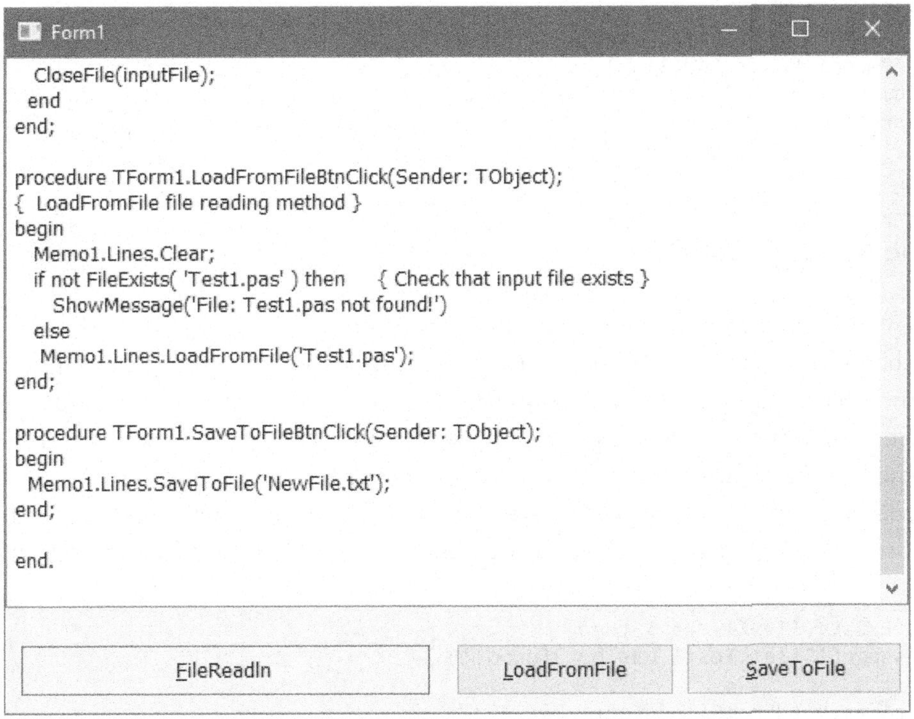

This uses text-file routines to read in a file (the file it reads happens to be this program's own source code) one line at a time. The lines are displayed in a Memo.

Apart from the declaration of the file type, which must be of the type `TextFile`, and the use of the `Readln` procedure, this closely resembles the code used previously to read data from a random access file:

textread

```
procedure TForm1.FileReadlnBtnClick(Sender: TObject);
var
    inputFile: TextFile;
    line: string;
begin
    Memo1.Lines.Clear;
    if not FileExists('Test1.pas') then
        ShowMessage('File: Test1.pas not found!')
    else
    begin
        AssignFile(inputFile, 'Test1.pas');
        Reset(inputFile);
        while not Eof(inputFile) do
        begin
            Readln(inputFile, line);
            Memo1.Lines.Add(line);
        end;
        CloseFile(inputFile);
    end
end;
```

'Built-in' File Access Routines

Just about every programming language supports both random access and text files. Delphi also has additional file-handling routines built into many of its visual components such as Memos. To load a file into the `Lines` of a Memo, you simply use the `LoadFromFile` method, using an existing file name as an argument. To save a file, you use the `SaveToFile` method using any valid file name as an argument.

The `LoadFromFileBtnClick` procedure in the *textread* project demonstrates the file-loading routine `LoadFromFile` to load the source code of the main unit in this project:

```
if not FileExists('Test1.pas') then
    ShowMessage('File: Test1.pas not found!')
else
    Memo1.Lines.LoadFromFile('Test1.pas');
```

The `SaveToFileBtnClick` procedure saves the contents of the Memo to a file named '*NewFile.txt*':

```
Memo1.Lines.SaveToFile('NewFile.txt');
```

The `LoadFromFile` and `SaveToFile` procedures each take care of all the tasks needed to assign, open, reset, rewrite, read or write and close a file. They are clearly much simpler to use than the traditional file-handling routines but they are only available for use with visual components such as Memos.

It is worth becoming comfortable with traditional text-file routines to give you more flexibility when processing text files. For example, there may be occasions when you want to process a file one character at a time – say to replace certain words in the file or to encrypt data.

Changing Characters in a Text File

For a simple example of how to encrypt a file one character at a time, load up the *encrypt_decrypt* project. This provides a button which, when clicked, reads in the file, `INFILENAME` (set to *'TextIO.pas'*) and writes out an encrypted version to the file `OUTFILENAME` (set to *'Encrypt.txt'*):

encrypt decrypt

```
var
    infile, outfile: TextFile;
    ch: AnsiChar;
begin
    if not FileExists(INFILENAME) then { Check that input file exists }
        ShowMessage('File: ' + INFILENAME + ' not found!')
    else
    begin
        AssignFile(infile, INFILENAME);
        Reset(infile);
        AssignFile(outfile, OUTFILENAME);
        Rewrite(outfile);
        while not Eof(infile) do
        begin
            Read(infile, ch);
            Write(outfile, AnsiChar(Ord(ch) + MAGICNUM));
        end;
        CloseFile(outfile);
        CloseFile(infile);
    end;
end;
```

You can check the contents of *Encrypt.txt* by loading it into any text editor. Although this file is a readable text file, its contents won't make any sense due to the fact that all the original characters have been altered. The encryption algorithm is extremely simple (and therefore not suitable for encrypting sensitive data!). It just adds a value, `MAGICNUM` (a `const` that is set to 17), to the ASCII code of the current character, `ch`:

```
AnsiChar(Ord(ch) + MAGICNUM)
```

Char or AnsiChar?

Here I use `AnsiChar` as the type for each character. This is because the actual data type of `char` (the range of characters which it supports) is different in differing versions of Delphi and Free Pascal. The `AnsiChar` type guarantees that byte size (8-bit) characters are used. That is the simplest solution for my rather simple encryption program.

Notice is that two files have been opened simultaneously. First the input file has been opened for reading; then the output file has been opened for writing:

```
AssignFile(infile, INFILENAME);
Reset(infile);
AssignFile(outfile, OUTFILENAME);
Rewrite(outfile);
```

A `while` loop reads through the input file until it reaches the end of the file, which is determined by the `Eof` function. Inside the loop, the input file is processed one character at a time, using `Read` and the is encrypted character is then written to the output file:

```
while not Eof(infile) do
begin
    Read(infile, ch);
    Write(outfile, AnsiChar(Ord(ch) + MAGICNUM));
end;
```

Finally, both files are closed:

```
CloseFile(outfile);
CloseFile(infile);
```

There, in a nutshell, you have all the essentials of text-file processing. To verify that the encryption has worked, I have also written a procedure to decrypt the encrypted file by subtracting the previously specified number from each character code read from the encrypted file:

```
Write(outfile, AnsiChar(Ord(ch) - MAGICNUM));
```

The decrypted file is saved to a file called '*Decrypt.txt*'. All being well, this should now contain the same text as the original file prior to its encryption.

File IO Routines

The following table shows the principal procedures and functions needed to open and close both typed (random access) and text files and to save or load data to and from them. Some routines, such as `Read` and `Write`, may take optional parameters. Only the simple form of these routines is shown below. You may want to search the Delphi Help system for more detailed information on these and other file-handling procedures.

		Text Files	Typed Files
`procedure AssignFile(FileVar; FileName);`	Associates the String, FileName, with the File Variable, FileVar .	Yes	Yes
`procedure CloseFile(FileVar);`	Closes the File, FileVar, which is open for reading or writing	Yes	Yes
`procedure Reset(FileVar);`	Opens an existing file.	Yes	Yes
`procedure Rewrite(FileVar);`	Creates and opens a new file.	Yes	Yes
`procedure Seek(FileVar; Position);`	Moves the current file position to a specified record.	No	Yes
`function EOF(FileVar) : boolean;`	Returns true if at end of file, else false.	Yes	Yes
`function FilePos(FileVar): Longint;`	Returns the current position within a file.	No	Yes
`function FileSize(FileVar): Longint;`	Returns the number of records in the file, FileVar.	No	Yes
`procedure Read(FileVar; V1)`	Reads a char from a text file or a record from a typed file into variable V1.	Yes	Yes
`procedure Readln(FileVar; aLine);`	Reads a line of text from a file.	Yes	No
`procedure Write(FileVar; V1);`	Writes a char to a text file or a typed item (e.g. a record) to a typed file.	Yes	Yes
`procedure Writeln(FileVar; aLine);`	Writes a line of text to a file	Yes	No

Chapter 7 – Object Orientation

In this chapter you'll discover the essential features of object orientation and learn how to use objects in your programs.

Most modern programming languages are, to some degree, object oriented. In object oriented programming ('OOP') languages, data items such as string and integers can be grouped with the functions and procedures that act upon them.

So a string variable might be grouped together with a procedure that sets the string to uppercase; an integer variable might be grouped together with some functions that do arithmetic on that integer. Each group of data-plus-functions is called an 'object'.

Object Oriented and Procedural Languages

Traditional Pascal is a 'procedural' language in which the fundamental building blocks are named blocks of code – procedures and functions. Object Pascal is an 'object oriented' language in which the fundamental building blocks are objects. An object is a bit like a record which may define multiple data items. But, unlike a record, an object may also contain its own procedures and functions.

Even though we haven't looked at object orientation in any depth up to now, we have, in fact, been using objects all the time. If you look at the code of the *cddbase* project from the last chapter, you'll see that `TForm1` is declared to be a `class`:

cddbase

```
TForm1 = class(TForm)
```

Classes and Objects

A class is the object oriented name for the *definition* of an object. Think of it as a blueprint. It is the 'design document' from which usable objects are created. In the real world, a car or a motorbike are usable objects which are created from the design specified by their blueprint. Think of it this way. I want to create several car objects so I first create the blueprint, which is the 'design document' for a car. The blueprint is, to a car, what the class is to an object in a computer program – it defines what a car (or an object) is:

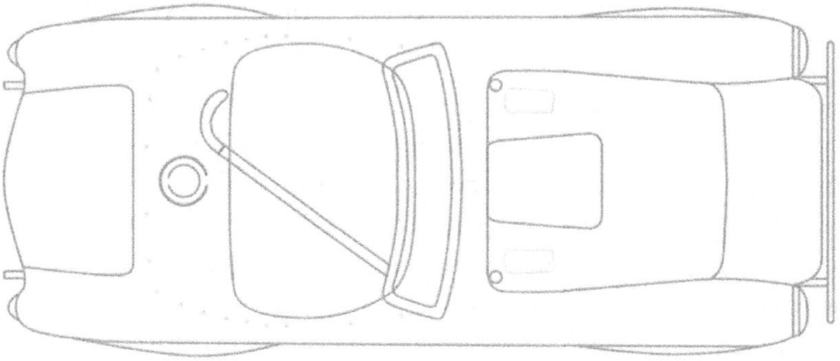

I can't drive the blueprint, of course. I can only drive a real car. In order to have a real car, one must be constructed from the blueprint. Similarly, in order to use a real object, I need to construct one based on its class definition. But why stop at one? I can create many cars from one blueprint. And I can create many objects from one class definition:

In a computer program, a form, a button or some other type of usable object is created from the design specified by its class definition. The top part of the `TForm1` class declaration contains the names and types of all the objects on the form, such as `CountBtn`, and also procedures or 'methods', such as `CountBtnClick`, that have been added automatically by Delphi when the visual designer was used to add components and event-handling methods:

cddbase

```
TForm1 = class(TForm)
    CountBtn: TButton;
    RecNumEd: TEdit;
    LoadBtn: TButton;
    Panel1: TPanel;
    Label1: TLabel;
    Label2: TLabel;
    Label3: TLabel;
    Label4: TLabel;
    FilePosLabel: TLabel;
    NameEd: TEdit;
    ArtistEd: TEdit;
    PriceEd: TEdit;
    SaveAsNewBtn: TButton;
    CDLabelEd: TEdit;
    Label5: TLabel;
    SaveChangesBtn: TButton;
    procedure CountBtnClick(Sender: TObject);
    procedure LoadBtnClick(Sender: TObject);
    procedure SaveAsNewBtnClick(Sender: TObject);
    procedure FormActivate(Sender: TObject);
    procedure SaveChangesBtnClick(Sender: TObject);
private
    { Private declarations }
public
    { Public declarations }
    procedure ShowCD(aCD: CD);
    function FieldsOK: boolean;
    procedure SaveCDRec(saveAsNew: boolean);
end;
```

Methods

Procedures or functions that are defined in classes and which are 'bound into' objects are generally referred to as 'methods'. Event-handling methods such as `CountBtnClick` and `LoadBtnClick` were created for me when I double-clicked the `OnClick` event for those button objects in the Events page of the designer's Object Inspector. But lower down the `TForm1` declaration, just beneath the keyword `public` I have added three of my own methods:

cddbase

```
public
    procedure ShowCD(aCD: CD);
    function FieldsOK: boolean;
    procedure SaveCDRec(SaveAsNew: boolean);
```

You can add your own methods to either the `public` or the `private` sections of a class declaration. If you add them to the `private` section, they won't be visible outside the current code unit. You must not add methods to the top section of a class declaration. That area is strictly reserved for the event-handling methods that are automatically generated and maintained by Delphi.

interface and implementation

The `interface` section of a Delphi unit is where constants, types, variables, procedures, and functions that are available to other units are declared. The `implementation` section is where you write the actual code of procedures and functions that are declared in the interface section. The `implementation` section can also declare constants, types, variables, procedures, and functions that are private to the unit. In other words, if you want code to be *public* (accessible outside the current unit) it must be declared after the `interface` keyword. If you want code to be *private* (so cannot be accessed by other units) it may be declared after the `implementation` keyword. Procedures and functions that are defined in the `implementation` section are only public if they are also declared in the `interface` section.

Having declared some `TForm1` methods in the `interface` section of this unit, I now have to write the code of those methods in the `implementation` section – that is, beneath the `implementation` keyword. To do this, I use the same syntax used by event-handler methods: that is, I precede each procedure or function name with the name of the class (here `TForm1`) in which they are declared, like this:

```
procedure TForm1.ShowCD(aCD: CD);
```

One advantage of creating your own `TForm1` methods is that they will have ready access to other methods and data of the `TForm1` object since they will be within the same scope. For example, within the `TForm1.ShowCD` method, my code can access component objects on the form, such as the `NameEd` edit box and assign values to its properties such as `Text` in this way:

```
NameEd.Text := name;
```

This would not be possible if `ShowCD` were a stand-alone procedure (not 'wrapped up' inside the `TForm1` class definition).

Why Object Orientation?

By now you may be asking yourself – what exactly is the *point* of Object Orientation? This is a topic that could be discussed at great length. For now, though, it is enough to concentrate on three things:

1) inheritance
2) encapsulation
3) reusability.

Inheritance

Objects can 'descend' from other objects in such a way that a descendant object automatically 'inherits' the data and behaviour of its ancestors. So if you've written some code in the ancestor, you won't need to write it all over again in the descendant.

For example, let's suppose you are writing a game that contains a `Monster` class (the blueprint from which your `Monster` objects will be created). You might write one procedure to move the monster around the world of your game and another procedure to make it growl.

When you later decide to write a `Troll` class, you realize that a `Troll` is a specific type of `Monster` so, instead of programming `Troll` objects from the ground up, you make `Troll` a descendent of `Monster`.

Your `Troll` objects automatically inherit the features of `Monster` (so they know how to move and growl). You would only need to add on features specific to Trolls – for example, their ability to hide under bridges and eat passers-by. You could create other descendants of `Monster` – let's say `Dragon`, which would inherit all the features of `Monster` and add on Dragon-specific features such as `fly` and `breath_fire`.

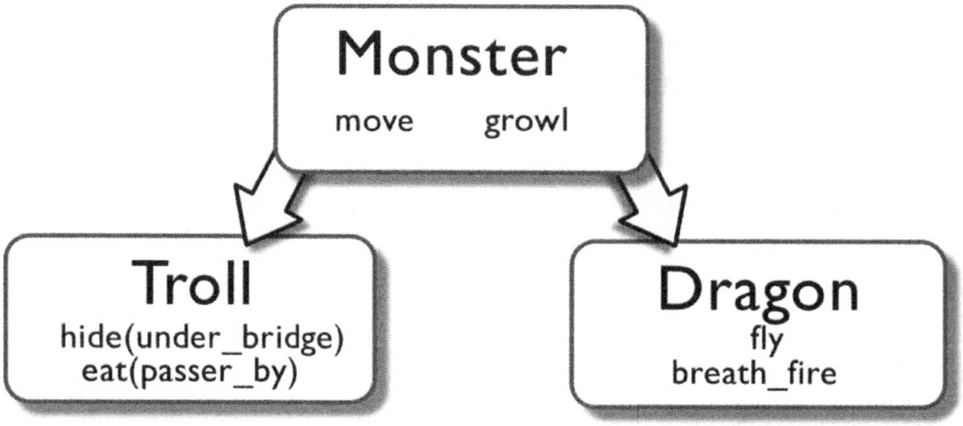

Encapsulation

'Encapsulation' describes the ability of objects to contain both data (just like *records*) and the procedures and functions (or 'methods') needed to act upon that data. In procedural programming, procedures may be scattered about all over the place in your code.

So even though the `growl` procedure will only ever be used by a `Monster` record, there is no intrinsic link between `Monster` and `growl` in your code. If you aren't careful you could accidentally use the `growl` procedure with a non-Monster object such as a `Treasure` – thereby causing the Elvish Sword to growl at unexpected moments!

If, however, `Monster` is an *object* rather than a *record*, you could bind the `growl` procedure into the object (that is, you would write that procedure as part of the `Monster` class definition).

As mentioned before, in object-oriented terminology, a procedure or function that is bound into an object or class is called a 'method' of that object or class. When it is bound into the `Monster` class, the `growl` method is only available to `Monster` objects or its descendants (such as `Troll` and `Dragon` objects). This makes for neater and safer code.

Reusability

Whenever possible, it is best to avoid writing the same code more than once. Object orientation lets you reuse your code creating multiple objects from that class. Moreover, by creating a 'class hierarchy' – that is, a 'family tree' of related classes – descendant classes have access to code that was defined by ancestor classes. Once again, this helps programmers to avoid unnecessarily repeating the same code.

Define Classes, Create Objects

While the *cddbase* project, which we looked at in Chapter 6, has some object orientated features (for example, its procedures are, in fact, 'methods' of the `TForm1` class), it doesn't go the whole hog. Notice that each `CD` data item is stored in a Pascal record which is declared in this way:

cddbase

```
CD = record
    name    : str30;
    artist  : str30;
    price   : double;
    cdlabel : str30;
end;
```

A record is not object orientated. Unlike an object, a record cannot contain methods or have descendants. In traditional Pascal (prior to the addition of object orientation) a record provided the only way of wrapping up several data fields into a single data-item.

It is very simple to change the `CD` record shown above into a class. Load up the *objects* project. You'll find that here have declared a class called `CDOb` which contains precisely the same fields as the `CD` record shown above:

objects

```
CDOb = class
    name    : str30;
    artist  : str30;
    price   : double;
    cdlabel : str30;
end;
```

Constructors

Appearances can be deceptive, however. While `CDOb` may *look* like a record, it cannot be *used* like a record. If this were a record, I could simply declare a variable and start assigning values to the fields. With a class there is an extra step involved: you must specifically *create* an *object* from the class definition. You do this by calling a special method called a 'constructor'. The standard Object Pascal constructor is named `Create`. So this is how I declare and create an object called `cd` of the type `CDOb`:

```
cd := CDOb.Create;    { This is Correct }
```

Note that you must specify the name of the *class*, `CDOb`, and not the name of the *object*, `cd`, when calling the constructor, `Create`. The reason for this is that the `cd` object doesn't exist until it *after* it has been created. So, even though the following expression is syntactically correct, it won't actually create a new object:

```
cd := cd.Create;    { This is Wrong! }
```

When the `Create` constructor is called, a chunk of computer memory is allocated big enough to hold an object of the specified type. An object variable, such as `cd` in this example, points to the location in memory of the object. The code in my project creates a fixed number of `CDOb` objects (here `ARRAYSIZE` is a constant that has the value 10):

```
for i := 1 to ARRAYSIZE do
begin
    cd := CDOb.Create;
    // more code goes here
end;
```

I have previously created four ten-slot arrays called `NAMEARRAY`, `ARTISTARRAY`, `PRICEARRAY` and `LABELARRAY` and I have initialized them with ten CD names, ten artist names, ten prices and ten record label names. For example, this is `NAMEARRAY`:

```
NAMEARRAY: StrArray = ('Greatest Hits','Big Ones','Golden Greats','Top Hits',
'All the Best', 'Fab Grooves','Unforgettable','Yeah!','Spiffing Tunes','Rare
Hits');
```

In the `FormCreate` procedure, my code assigns values from the pre-defined arrays to each newly created object. It does this by setting up a `for` loop to count from 1 to `ARRAYSIZE`.

At each turn through the loop, the loop-counter variable, `i`, is used to retrieve the item at each matching index of each of my four arrays. The code creates a new `CDOb` object, `cd`, and initializes the fields of that object with the data from the arrays:

```
for i := 1 to ARRAYSIZE do
  begin
    cd := CDOb.Create;
    cd.name := NAMEARRAY[i];
    cd.artist := ARTISTARRAY[i];
    cd.price := PRICEARRAY[i];
    cd.cdlabel := LABELARRAY[i];
    obArray[i] := cd;
  end;
```

The last line inside the loop (`obArray[i] := cd;`), adds the new object, `cd`, to a specific slot (the current index of the loop variable `i`) in `obArray`, which has been previously declared to be an array of `CDOb` objects:

```
obArray : array[1..ARRAYSIZE] of CDOb;
```

Once the slots of the `obArray` have been filled with `CDOb` objects, I can access any object by specifying its array index. I can then access the values of each object's fields using dot-notation just as I would access the fields of a record.

You can see how this is done in the `ShowObsBtnClick` method. This iterates through the array using a `for` loop. At each index, `i`, it assigns the `CDOb` object to a local `CDOb` variable named `cd`:

```
cd := ObArray[i];
```

It then obtains the values of each field using dot-notation:

```
cd.name {etc.}
```

The values of the field of each object in the array are concatenated into a string which is then displayed in a line of `Memo1`.

```
Memo1.Lines.add('[' + IntToStr(i) + '] ' + cd.name + ', ' +
          cd.artist + ', ' + FloatToStrF(cd.price, ffCurrency, 2, 2) +
          ', ' + cd.cdlabel);
```

You can see the results by running the program and clicking the '*Show All*' button:

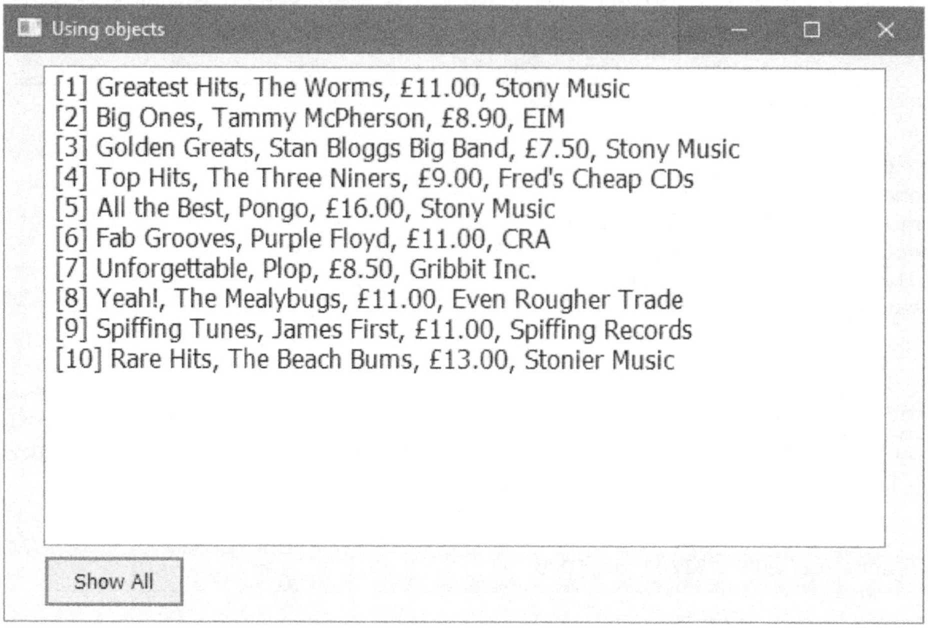

Freeing Objects

Recall that I said earlier that when an object is created, its constructor sets aside some memory for it. That memory will be reserved ('allocated') for the object until your code specifically deallocates it. In order to deallocate memory you should call a special method called a 'destructor'. The normal destructor is named `Destroy`. However, it is recommended that you dispose of objects by calling a different method, called `Free`, which itself calls the `Destroy` destructor. The reason for this is that the `Free` method succeeds even if an object is `nil` (in Object Pascal, the value `nil` may be assigned to an object which has no specific value). The `Destroy` destructor will not succeed when an object is `nil`.

Unlike the constructor, which is called using the class name, the destructor (or its intermediary method, `Free`), is called using the *object* name, not the class name. This is how I would dispose of the `cd` object and free up its memory:

```
cd.Free;
```

In the present project, I need to iterate over all the objects stored in the array `obArray`, freeing each object in turn. To do this, I use a `for` loop to free the object at each index of the array:

```
for i := 1 to ARRAYSIZE do
    obArray[i].Free;
```

In the *objects* project, I free the objects in the `FormClose` method which executes when the application is shutting down. This is not strictly necessary since the objects' memory will, in any case, be deallocated when the program ends. However, it is a good habit explicitly to free all objects that you created and no harm is done by doing so here.

Take Care When Freeing Objects

There are two important rules to follow when freeing objects:

1) Only free objects that you are sure you won't need again.

In the present project, the objects are freed prior to closing the application, so I can be sure they are finished with. In other applications, you might free objects at other times – for example when an object (a `CD` item, say, or a `Treasure`) is deleted from a database or a game, or when you need to destroy all objects in an array prior to adding a new set of objects.

2) Never try to use an object that has been freed.

Once you have called an object's destructor, that object no longer exists. The memory it was previously allocated may already have been put to some other use. If you try to access that object, you risk crashing your program!

Saving Objects

Incidentally, you may be wondering how to save the data in your objects to a file on disk. This is a bit trickier than saving data from records since you cannot simply declare a file of objects. There are various ways of dealing with the problem. Experienced programmers may employ a technique called 'serialization' whereby each object is responsible for saving its own data. Serialization is a powerful technique that lets you save data from complex 'networks' of objects.

In some languages, (such as Java and C#) serialization is easy to do. In Object Pascal, however, it can be a bit trickier. I'll look at serialization in Chapter 10. However, if you want a way of saving data from a list of fairly simple objects like my array of `CDOb` objects, you could copy the data from each object into the fields of a compatible record and then save the records to a typed file. You can find an example of this in the *objects2* sample project.

objects2

```
procedure TForm1.SaveBtnClick(Sender: TObject);
var
    recFile: file of CDRec;
    i: integer;
    aRec: CDRec;
begin
    AssignFile(recFile, FILENAME);
    Rewrite(recFile);
    for i := 1 to ARRAYSIZE do
    begin
       { if object variable is nil then save a record with '' or 0 value fields }
        if obArray[i] = nil then
        begin
            aRec.name := '';
            aRec.artist := '';
            aRec.price := 0.0;
            aRec.cdlabel := '';
        end
       { else map object's fields onto a record and save the record }
        else
        begin
            aRec.name := obArray[i].name;
            aRec.artist := obArray[i].artist;
            aRec.price := obArray[i].price;
            aRec.cdlabel := obArray[i].cdlabel;
        end;
        Write(recFile, aRec);
    end;
    CloseFile(recFile);
end;
```

Chapter 8 – Class Hierarchies

In this chapter we find out how to create hierarchies of related objects, how to hide data and how to create 'properties' to access variables.

I want to write a program to maintain a catalogue of books. I want it to be able to store the details of three types of book: *General Fiction, Reference Book* and *Horror Book*. My first attempt at this can be found in the *bookobs* project. The user interface of this program includes text fields and drop-down 'combo box' lists so that, when adding details of a book, you can enter the book title and author for all book types. A Reference Book also lets you enter details of the 'reference type', while a Horror Book lets you enter a 'gore score' value between 0 and 10 indicating its scariness.

Before looking at the code, run the application to see how it works. Leave the combo box set to '*General Fiction*'. Enter the book name and author name shown below for the two text fields at the top-right of the form:

Book Title: Bleak House
Author: Charles Dickens

Click the '*Add Book*' button. The List Box will display this:

```
CONSTRUCTOR: BookOb.Create'
```

This message indicates that the constructor method `BookOb.Create` was called and a new `BookOb` object has been created. View the details of the object by clicking the '*Show Books*' button.

Now select '*Horror*' from the combo box. Notice that a second combo box appears, listing a range of 'gore score' values. Enter these details:

Book Title: The Shining
Author: Stephen King
Gore Score: 7

Now click '*Add Book*'.

You will see that this time, two constructors have been called:

```
CONSTRUCTOR: BookOb.Create
CONSTRUCTOR: HorrorBookOb.Create
```

Now select *'Reference'* from the book-type combo box. This time a different field pops up in which you can enter a description of the type of reference book. Add these details:

Book Title: Aquarium Care
Author: G. Sterba
Reference Type: Fish

Click *'Add Book'*.
This time, these two constructors are called:

```
CONSTRUCTOR: BookOb.Create
CONSTRUCTOR: RefBookOb.Create
```

Click *'Show Books'*. You should see a listing of the three books you've entered:

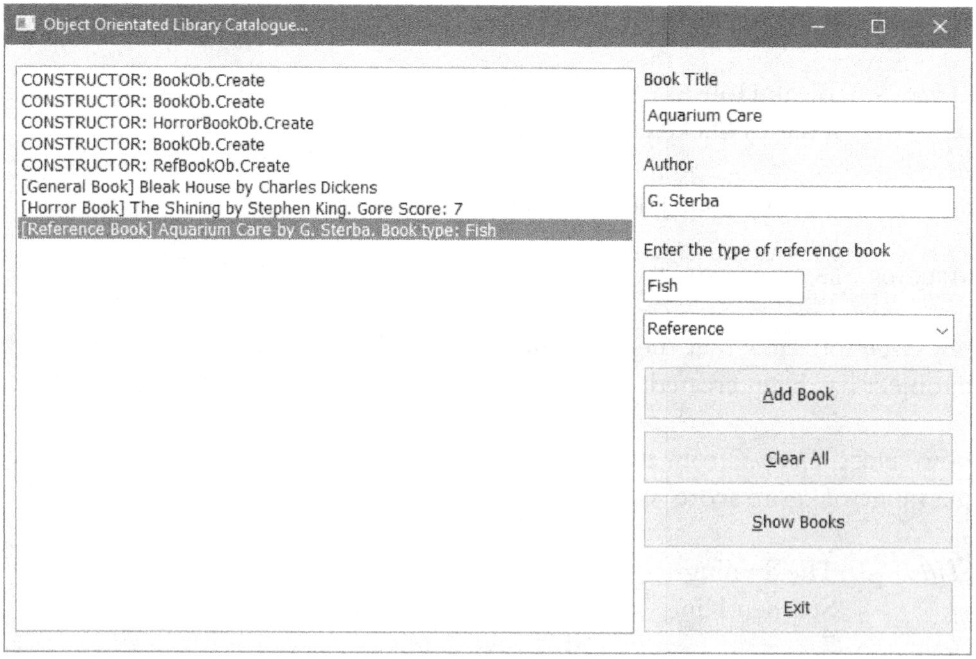

The important thing to notice is that all three books have two things in common: a *name* and an *author*. However, the Horror Book and the Reference Book add on their own special features: a *Gore Score* in one case, a *Book Type* in the other.

Inheritance

If you think about it, you'll see that these three types of book form a clear hierarchy. All books have a name and an author, so we can create a basic `BookOb` with those two elements. Having created such a `BookOb`, we can create descendant objects for more specialized *types* of books.

Remember that descendant objects automatically inherit the data and behavior of their ancestors. So if `HorrorBookOb` and `RefBookOb` descend from `BookOb` they will automatically inherit the `name` and `author` fields. As a result, they need to implement only those things which *differ* from their ancestor.

Close down the application and turn to the *books.pas* unit. Here you will see this class definition of `BookOb`:

bookobs (books.pas)

```
BookOb = class(TObject)
    name   : bkstr;
    author : bkstr;
    function Describe : bkstr;
    constructor Create(aName, anAuthor : bkstr);
    destructor Destroy; override;
end;
```

Notice that I have placed the name of the ancestor class of `BookOb` between parentheses:

```
BookOb = class(TObject)
```

In fact, if you omit a specific class name, Object Pascal automatically makes your class a descendant of `TObject`.

TObject

In Object Pascal, `TObject` is the ultimate ancestor of all other objects and components. It deals with features required for the creation and destruction of objects and other essential behaviour.

My other two classes descend from `BookOb`:

```
HorrorBookOb = class(BookOb)
RefBookOb = class(BookOb)
```

As you can see from their definitions, each of these descendant classes defines a single field. `HorrorBookOb` defines an integer called `gorescore` while the `RefBookOb` class defines a string (a of the `BookString` type which I have previously defined to have a length of 70 characters) called `reftype`. Due to the fact that these classes are descendants of `BookOb`, they also implicitly include the two fields defined by their ancestor class `BookOb` – that is, `name` and `author`. These, then are my three class definitions:

```
BookOb = class(TObject)
    name   : BookString;
    author : BookString;
    function Describe : BookString;
    constructor Create(aName, anAuthor : BookString);
    destructor Destroy; override;
end;

HorrorBookOb = class(BookOb)
    gorescore : integer;
    function Describe : BookString;
    constructor Create(aName, anAuthor:BookString; aGoreScore:GoreRating);
    destructor Destroy; override;
end;

RefBookOb = class(BookOb)
    reftype : BookString;
    function Describe : BookString;
    constructor Create(aName, anAuthor, aRefType : BookString);
    destructor Destroy; override;
end;
```

These three classes demonstrate one of the most important features of Object Orientation: *inheritance*. By inheriting features from their ancestor class `BookOb` the two descendant classes `HorrorBookOb` and `RefBookOb` have avoided any necessity to re-implement existing features (here, that's the `name` and `author` of each book). You could go on to create further descendants of these classes if you wished. For example, you might create more specialized versions of `RefBookOb`:

```
ScienceBookOb = class(RefBookOb)
LanguageBookOb = class(RefBookOb)
```

ScienceBookOb might include an extra field named subject to indicate whether this is a physics, chemistry, biology book and so on. LanguageBookOb might have two extra fields one called language (French, German, Japanese etc.) and the other called level (Beginner, Intermediate or Advanced). I've decided to restrict my sample project to just three classes for simplicity. However, you might want to see if you can modify my project by adding the additional classes mentioned above.

Encapsulation

Now let me turn to the procedures and functions defined by the three book classes. As mentioned previously, in OOP jargon, the procedures and functions that 'belong' to specific classes are usually called 'methods'. Each of my classes declares three methods called Describe, Create and Destroy. Create and Destroy are preceded by the keywords constructor and destructor. The Describe method, on the other hand, is just a normal function that returns a BookString.

```
function Describe : BookString;
constructor Create(aName, anAuthor : BookString);
destructor Destroy; override;
```

The Create constructor and the Destroy destructor are already implemented by Delphi's TObject class.

Overriding Destroy

Notice that Destroy is followed by the reserved word override. This is required because Destroy is a 'virtual' method. The significance of this is explained later in this chapter.

By wrapping up both data and methods inside the classes themselves, this project has implemented another major feature of OOP – *encapsulation*. And by redefining three methods, Describe, Create and Destroy, our classes also implement another feature of object oriented programming – *polymorphism*.

Polymorphism

In simple terms, *polymorphism* describes the ability of different classes to implement methods with the same name. So the Cat class and the Dog class could each have a method called `Talk`. The `Cat`'s `Talk` method would display "Meow!", while the `Dog`'s `Talk` method would display "Woof!". While the term 'polymorphism' is often used in academic texts on Object Orientation, in my view the term can make simple ideas seem more complicated. It is not a term that I will use much in this book.

Create Constructors

The version of the `Create` constructor for `BookOb` objects takes two parameters. These are the data items used to initialize the fields of each object when it is created:

```
constructor BookOb.Create(aName, anAuthor : BookString);
begin
    inherited Create;
    name := aName;
    author := anAuthor;
end;
```

Here the parameters `aName` and `anAuthor` initialize the fields `name` and `author` respectively. Prior to doing this `BookOb.Create` calls the constructor of its immediate ancestor or 'base' class:

```
inherited Create;
```

When you are writing your own constructors, a call to the constructor of the base class should be the first statement. The `inherited` keyword is an instruction to call the specified method, here the `Create` constructor, of the current class's ancestor. This ensures that the ancestor's data is correctly initialized prior to initializing any additional fields in the descendant.

If the ancestor's `Create` method takes some parameters, these must be used. You can see an example of this in `HorrorBookOb.Create`. The ancestor of this object is `BookOb`. So the first statement in the `HorrorBookOb` constructor calls the `BookOb` constructor and passes to it the two required arguments:

```
inherited Create(aName, anAuthor);
```

So when a `HorrorBookOb` is created, the constructor of `BookOb` is called and this then calls the constructor of its own ancestor, `TObject`. You can verify the order in which the constructors of `BookOb` and its descendants are called by running the application once more and paying close attention to the messages displayed in the Memo when each new object is created.

inherited

It is also permissible to call an inherited method without specifying the name of the ancestor method, like this:

```
inherited;
```

When used in this way `inherited` invokes the ancestor method with the same name as the current method and it passes to the ancestor method the same parameters which were passed to the current method. This is clearly a more concise syntax for calling inherited methods but it is not as clear as the longer form inch which both the method name and its arguments are required.

Incidentally, in this sample project, I have put the similarly-named methods and class destructors close to one another in order to make them easy to locate and compare. For example, in *books.pas* these three destructor methods are placed after one another:

```
destructor BookOb.Destroy;
destructor HorrorBookOb.Destroy;
destructor RefBookOb.Destroy;
```

It is normally better practice to put all the code of each class into a consecutive block rather than mixing up code belonging to different classes. You will find an example of this in the *game01* project in Chapter 10.

In fact, in real-world projects, it would be better to put the code of each class into its own code file so that *CatUnit.pas* would contain all the code of the `Cat` class (say) while *DogUnit.pas* would contain all the code of the `Dog` class – and so on. You will find an example of this in the *game02* project in Chapter 10.

Destructors

Normally you will only implement your own destructors when you need to free up any memory that's been allocated inside your objects. For example, if one of the data fields inside your `BookOb` were itself an object, you would need to `Free` that object in `BookOb`'s destructor.

In fact, my `BookOb` class is rather straightforward and it does not really need its own destructor. Nevertheless, I have added a destructor to provide an example of how this is done. As you can see, just as I called the inherited *constructor* in the `Create` constructor, so I call the inherited *destructor* in the `Destroy` destructor:

```
inherited Destroy;
```

The difference is that the call to the inherited constructor is made *before* initializing any fields. But the call to the inherited destructor is made *after* clearing the fields, typically by freeing any objects.

Free or Destroy?

Remember that when destroying objects, you should generally call the `Free` method rather than the `Destroy` destructor. As explained in Chapter 7, this is recommended when disposing of objects because `Free` tests whether or not an object variable is equal to `nil` (that is, if it doesn't actually point to an object). If it *is* `nil`, the `Free` method does nothing, so no attempt is made to destroy an object that doesn't exist! If it is *not* `nil`, it calls the `Destroy` destructor.

Methods with the same Names

Look at the `Describe` function in each of my three book classes. This returns a formatted string showing the values of the fields in each object. `BookOb.Describe` returns this:

```
result := Format('[General Book] %s by %s', [name,author]);
```

`HorrorBookOb` and `RefBookOb` return different sets of values due to the fact that these classes define different data fields.

```
    // HorrorBookOb.Describe
result := Format('[Horror Book] %s by %s. Gore Score: %d',
                 [name, author, gorescore]);
    // RefBookOb.Describe
result := Format('[Reference Book] %s by %s. Book type: %s',
                 [name, author, reftype]);
```

As long as you only ever called `Describe` from an object of the appropriate type of class, the correct version of the `Describe` method will run. However, sometimes you may not know in advance, which type of object you are dealing with. I show an example of this problem in the *bookprob* project.

Polymorphism Revisited

Writing multiple methods called `Describe` in different classes is an example of polymorphism – which I mentioned earlier in this chapter. Don't worry about the terminology. 'Polymorphism' is a fancy word for a simple idea.

The *bookprob* project contains the same code as the previous project, *bookobs*, apart from one method. Find `TForm1.ShowObList` which is at the top of the implementation section. This method is called when the user clicks the '*Show Books*' button. It scrolls through the objects in a list of objects called `obList`:

bookprob

```
procedure TForm1.ShowObList;
{ casts an object to BookOb then calls the Describe method }
{ Help! There's something wrong!!! }
var
    i: integer;
    s: BookString;
begin
    if obList.Count = 0 then
        ListBox1.Items.Add('No books in the list!')
    else
        for i := 0 to obList.Count - 1 do
            ListBox1.Items.Add(BookOb(obList.Items[i]).Describe);
end;
```

Here `obList` is a collection object of the type `TList`. This is more flexible than an array since it can contain varying numbers of objects rather than being restricted to a fixed set of elements. Just like any other object, `obList` has to be specifically created and destroyed. It is created in the `TForm1.FormCreate` method which executes when the application is first loaded:

```
procedure TForm1.FormCreate(Sender: TObject);
begin
    { Create a TList called ObList when the main form is created }
    obList := TList.Create;
end;
```

It is destroyed ('freed') in the `TForm1.FormClose` method which executes when the application is shut down:

```
procedure TForm1.FormClose(Sender: TObject; var Action: TCloseAction);
begin
    FreeObs;     { Free the objects in the ObList, then...      }
    obList.Free; { Free the ObList when the main form is closed }
end;
```

Casting Types

Since any type of object can potentially be contained in `obList`, we must tell the compiler to treat each item as a `BookOb` (this is called 'casting' or 'coercion'), in order that we can call the `Describe` method, which is only available to `BookOb` and its descendants.

To cast an object to `BookOb` I have to enter the class name, `BookOb`, followed by an opening parenthesis, then the object to be cast (in this case, an object at index `i` of `obList.Items`), and finally a closing parenthesis:

```
BookOb(obList.Items[i])
```

Then I append the name of the method using the familiar dot-notation:

```
BookOb(obList.Items[i]).Describe
```

Try this out. Run the application. Add one *General Fiction* book, one *Reference* book and one *Horror* book. Then click the '*Show Books*' button. You'll find there is a problem. Each book describes itself as a General Book. This is not at all what I had intended:

Testing Object Types

If you load up the *bookobs* project once again, you will see that this has a different version of `TForm1.ShowObList`:

bookobs

```
procedure TForm1.ShowObList;
var
    i: integer;
    s: BookString;
begin
    if obList.Count = 0 then
        ListBox1.Items.Add('No books in the list!')
    else
        for i := 0 to obList.Count - 1 do
        begin
            if TObject(obList.Items[i]) is HorrorBookOb then
                s := HorrorBookOb(obList.Items[i]).Describe
            else if TObject(obList.Items[i]) is RefBookOb then
                s := RefBookOb(obList.Items[i]).Describe
            else
                s := BookOb(obList.Items[i]).Describe;
            ListBox1.Items.Add(s);
        end;
end;
```

Recall that in the *bookprob* project, the code iterated over the list, casting each object to `BookOb`. This works because `BookOb` is the 'parent' or 'base class' of `HorrorBookOb` and `RefBookOb`, so all three classes are indeed 'types of' `BookOb`. Unfortunately, since they are all treated as instances of the base class, `BookOb`, the version of the `Describe` method that is called is always the one defined for the `BookOb` class – never the version defined for `HorrorBookOb` or `RefBookOb`:

bookprob

```
for i := 0 to obList.Count - 1 do
    ListBox1.Items.Add(BookOb(obList.Items[i]).Describe);
```

By contrast, code in the `for` loop of the *bookobs* project goes one generation back up the class hierarchy in order to cast each object in `obList` to `TObject`.

```
TObject(ObList.Items[i])
```

I use a special operator, `is`, to test whether each object is derived from a specific class. The code here tests to see if the current object is a `HorrorBookOb`:

```
if TObject(ObList.Items[i]) is HorrorBookOb
```

If this test succeeds, my code casts the object to the `HorrorBookOb` class and then calls the `Describe` method. I can be sure that this will now be the version of the `Describe` method that is implemented by `HorrorBookOb` rather than the version implemented by `BookOb`:

```
if TObject(ObList.Items[i]) is HorrorBookOb then
    s := HorrorBookOb(ObList.Items[i]).Describe
```

A similar test and cast is used to call the version of `Describe` appropriate to `RefBookOb` and `BookOb` objects. If you run the application and enter books of various types, you will see that these `is` tests have fixed the problem I had in the *bookprob* project, so that this time the version of `Describe` defined for each *specific* type of object is called:

```
CONSTRUCTOR: BookOb.Create
CONSTRUCTOR: BookOb.Create
CONSTRUCTOR: RefBookOb.Create
CONSTRUCTOR: BookOb.Create
CONSTRUCTOR: HorrorBookOb.Create
[General Book] Happy Times by Slibbet van Dobrett
[Reference Book] The GripFerret by S T Grip. Book type: General
[Horror Book] Nasty Things by Damon Slither. Gore Score: 10
```

So clearly this test-and-cast approach works. Even so, this technique is unsatisfactory for the simple reason that the more different types of objects I define, the more `is` tests I have to scatter around in my code. This is not a big problem in a program with just three classes. But if I were to define a class hierarchy with dozens of different classes, all those tests and casts would quickly make my code verbose and complicated. Since one of the aims of Object Orientation is increased simplicity, this surely can't be right!

Virtual Methods

Let's see what we can do to simplify this code. Load up the *bookobs2* project. Find the `ShowObList` method. This time all the `is` tests have been removed and the simpler version of the code used in the *bookprob* project has been reinstated. Once again, I cast each object to the `BookOb` class and call the `Describe` method:

```
BookOb(ObList.Items[i]).Describe
```

This makes the for loop really simple. No tests, no casts. It just counts through the elements in obList and adds the string returned from the Describe method to ListBox1:

bookobs2

```
for i := 0 to obList.Count - 1 do
    ListBox1.Items.Add(BookOb(obList.Items[i]).Describe);
```

If you run the application, you'll find that the correct version of Describe is called for each type of object. When a HorrorBookOb describes itself, it includes its gorescore. When a RefBookOb describes itself it includes its reftype. But how come this works correctly here whereas exactly the same code did *not* work correctly in the *bookprob* project?

The answer can be found in the class definitions. This is how the Describe method has been declared in the BookOb class:

```
function Describe : BookString; virtual;
```

The two descendant classes, HorrorBookOb and RefBookOb, declare the Describe method in this way:

```
function Describe : BookString; override;
```

Overriding Methods

If you append the directive virtual to a method declaration you can subsequently redefine that method in descendant classes by appending the override directive – and that is what I have done here. This instructs the compiler to wait until the program is run before deciding which version of the method to call. Normally a compiler makes this decision at the time the program is compiled. The link from the method-call to the executable code of the method itself is compiled into your program and cannot be changed.

In the current application, Describe is a *virtual* method in the ancestor class (BookOb) and it is *overridden* in its two descendant classes. Even though the ShowObList method has been obliged to cast objects to the base BookOb type, the program calls the version of Describe that is appropriate to each *specific type* of object. This is because the link from the BookOb object to the virtual Describe method is *not* fixed in place when the program is compiled; that link is only made when the method is called during program execution. So in the for loop, even though the elements are cast to the ancestor BookOb type, when the

`Describe` method is called, the running program discovers that `Describe` is a *virtual* method so it checks to see if the method has been overridden for the specific object type. It sees that the specific object type is a descendant of `BookOb` and finds that it has an *overridden* `Describe` method, so *that* is the method that it calls. Now a `HorrorBookOb` will indeed use its own `Describe` method rather than that of its ancestor `BookOb`.

Understanding Virtual/Overridden Methods

Overriding virtual methods is a tricky concept to grasp at first. Probably the best way to understand what's going on is to try writing your own virtual methods. As an exercise you might want to create a `Bird` class and then write a couple of descendant classes: `Turkey` and `Chicken`. Give each bird in the hierarchy a different `Squawk` method. Make this *virtual* and then *override* it. Your aim should be to make simple `Bird` objects go *tweet* (that is, display the string 'Tweet' when the `Squawk` method is called) whereas `Chicken` objects go *cluck* and `Turkey` objects go *gobble-gobble*. Verify that you understand the difference when methods are virtual and overridden and when they are not.

Notice, by the way, that the standard destructor, `Destroy`, is a virtual method which is overridden in each descendant class. See if you can figure out why this is necessary. Recall that you normally destroy objects by calling the `Free` method and that this method itself calls `Destroy`. Imagine what would happen if `Destroy` weren't virtual? Would `Free` call the correct version of the destructor?

Properties

You should, by now, be familiar with the properties that appear in the Properties panel of the Delphi visual designer. These let you set attributes of buttons, memos and other controls either by entering them into a field in the Properties panel or by assigning values in your Pascal code. For example, to put 'Hello world' into a text box called `MyTextBox` you would set its `Text` property like this:

```
MyTextBox.Text := 'Hello world';
```

Properties are not restricted for use by visual objects. You can also define properties for your own custom classes. To see how this is done, load the *properties* project. This contains a new version of the `BookOb` class which includes two properties called `Name` and `Author`:

properties

```
BookOb = class
strict private
    _name: BookString;
    _author: BookString;
    procedure AddAuthor(anAuthor: BookString);
public
    property Name: BookString read _name write _name;
    property Author: BookString read _author write AddAuthor;
    function Describe: BookString;
    constructor Create;
    destructor Destroy; override;
end;
```

Notice that the variables `_name` and `_author` have been placed in a section of the class beneath the keywords `strict private`. This ensures that only a `BookOb` object is able to access those variables. If I were to write some code – say in a *ButtonClick* method – to try to set a value for `_name`, the compiler wouldn't let me:

```
aBook._name := 'Bleak House';    // This is an error!
```

Visibility Specifiers

Here `strict` and `private` are keywords that enforce the 'visibility' rules which apply to any 'members' of the class (its variables and methods) that follow – up until some other keyword begins a section with different visibility rules.

The keyword `private` on its own makes the members visible only to the current class *and any other code in the same unit.* If I had defined the `BookOb` class in its own separate code unit, the keyword `private` would be sufficient to ensure that no non-`BookOb` code could access its private members.

Since my `BookOb` class shares a unit with the code of my form, `TForm1`, I have had to precede `private` with `strict` to ensure that only code belonging to `BookOb` objects (and not to `TForm1`) can access `BookOb` private members. Don't worry too much about all these keywords. The two most important are `public` and `private`. However, it's worth recognizing others when you see them.

Summary of visibility specifiers

`public`	members have no access restrictions.
`protected`	members are accessible within the unit where its class is declared and by any descendent class in any unit.
`private`	visible only in the unit where it is declared.
`strict private`	members are visible only to the class itself.
`strict protected`	members are visible only to the class and its descendants.

Reading and Writing Properties

Since the `_name` variable is private, I need to provide some way in which its value can be accessed. As I want to be able both to get and set its value, I need to provide both read and write accessors. A `read` accessor lets me get the current value of the variable; a `write` accessor lets me set or assign a new value. This is how I've done that:

```
property Name : BookString read _name write _name;
```

What this says is: create a property called `Name` such that when a new value is assigned to that property, *write* (that is, 'assign') this value to the `_name` variable, and when the current value of the `Name` property is requested, *read* the value from the `_name` variable.

But, given the fact that the public `Name` property provides you with full access to the private `_name` variable, you might reasonably ask: so why not just make `_name` public? The advantage of using properties instead of variables is that they give you a finer degree of control over the level of access that you wish to allow.

Read-only Properties

Let's suppose that you want people to be able to retrieve the names of books but you want to make sure that they cannot assign new names to them. In order to do that you would give `read` access but no `write` access to the `Name` property like this:

```
property Name : BookString read _name;
```

Now this assignment would not be allowed:

```
aBook.Name := NameEdit.Text;
```

Write-only Properties

If, on the other hand, you wanted to allow the user to assign a new name but not to retrieve its value (maybe you want to make sure the `_name` string can only be used by the `Describe` method to ensure that a nicely formatted book description is returned), then you could give `write` access to `Name` but no `read` access, like this:

```
property Name : BookString write _name;
```

Now this would not be allowed:

```
Caption := aBook.Name;
```

Method Properties

Properties aren't restricted to accessing variables. They can also be used to delegate access to a named method. For an example of this, see the `Author` property:

```
property Author : BookString read _author write AddAuthor;
```

This delegates write access to the `AddAuthor` method. This is the code of that method:

properties

```
procedure BookOb.AddAuthor(anAuthor: BookString);
var
    trimmedAuthor: BookString;
begin
    trimmedAuthor := Trim(anAuthor);
    if trimmedAuthor = '' then
        trimmedAuthor := 'Anon'
    else if pos(' ', trimmedAuthor) = 0 then
        trimmedAuthor := '[First name unknown] ' + trimmedAuthor;
    _author := trimmedAuthor;
end;
```

When the user assigns a value to the `Author` property, that value is passed as an argument to the `AddAuthor` method. This method begins by trimming the `anAuthor` parameter (that is, removing white space from the start and end of the string). It assigns this to the local variable, `trimmedAuthor`. It then tests this variable. If it is an empty string, it sets `trimmedAuthor` to `'Anon'`.

If there is no space separator character (that is if the position of the `' '` character in `trimmedAuthor`, as returned by the `pos` function, is `0`) then it sets `trimmedAuthor` to `'[First name unknown] ' + trimmedAuthor`. This would occur if, for example, the user entered `'Dickens'` instead of `'Charles Dickens'`. And finally the `_author` variable is assigned the value of `trimmedAuthor`.

So you can see that, even though the `Author` property can be assigned a new value using the same syntax which you would use to assign a value to a variable, the property's `write` accessor method does quite a lot of work before actually assigning that value to `_author`. If you wish, you could also write a method to handle the `read` access of `Author`. This method would need to be a function that returns data of the appropriate type.

How to add a Method Property

As an exercise, try adding a method `GetAuthor` as the `read` property of `Author`. You can try this on your own or follow the instructions below. First you will need to enter the function declaration into the `strict private` section of `BookOb`:

```
function GetAuthor: BookString;
```

Then write the `GetAuthor` function in the implementation section of the code unit – here the function returns `_author` in uppercase:

```
function BookOb.GetAuthor: BookString;
begin
    result := AnsiUpperCase(_author);
end;
```

Now specify the function name in the `Author` property:

```
property Author : BookString read GetAuthor write AddAuthor;
```

To test this property, add this to the `Button1Click` method:

```
Caption := aBook.Author;
```

If you have rewritten the `Author` property in the way I suggest, this is what you will see if you enter 'Oliver Twist' and 'Charles Dickens' into the two text fields, then click the '*Assign Name and Author*' and '*Show Book*' buttons. Notice that the read property of `Author` displays the author name in uppercase in the form's caption bar:

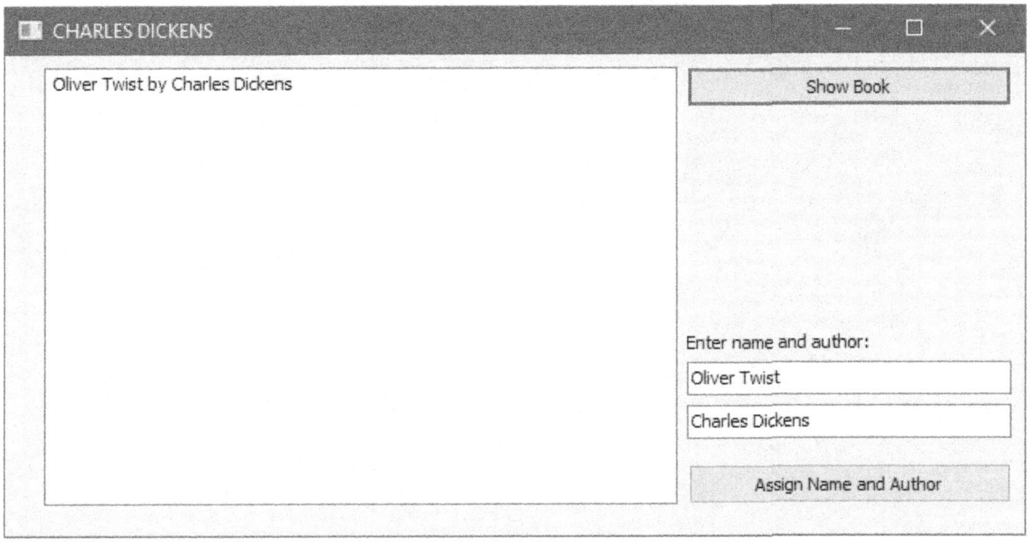

Properties give you control over data access. They allow you not only to check for valid data but also to process that data (for example, by trimming a string or changing its case). Moreover, if you need to change the way that data is accessed when you rewrite your code at a future date, you can do so easily. If you allow direct access to variables, on the other hand, you cannot easily make changes since that would risk 'breaking' any existing code that relies on having direct access to an object's internal data. As a general principle, data-hiding is strongly recommended.

Data-hiding

Data-hiding is complementary to 'encapsulation'. What, after all, is the point of making data (variables) *internal* to an object if the world outside that object has direct access to that data? It is better to create your objects as 'black boxes' whose internal structure is invisible to the world outside. The first step towards accomplishing this is to hide an object's data (make it `private`) and provide clearly-defined means of access (`public` methods) to manipulate that data.

Chapter 9 – Errors, Exceptions and Bugs

Your program works fine. Then you give it to the user and it crashes! In this chapter we look at ways of protecting your programs against unexpected errors.

A good programmer always tries to anticipate any possible errors that might occur and fix them before a program is released to the user. There are, however, some occasions when it is practically impossible to know if an error will occur until the program is being run! For example, the *cddbase* project (which we first saw in Chapter 6) asks the user to enter the number of a record into the `RecNumEd` text field. The `LoadBtnClick` procedure then tries to convert this text (a string) into an integer as follows:

```
recNum := StrToInt(RecNumEd.Text);
```

However, we can't be certain that the user will enter a string that can, in fact, be converted to an integer. For example, you won't be able to convert an alphabetic character such `'A'`, or a floating point number such as `5.5`. What's more, if the text box is left empty, the conversion will fail. An error of this sort necessarily breaks the flow of your program's execution. Object Pascal responds by 'throwing an exception'. An exception is a special type of object that contains information about the error.

Automatic Exception-Handling

Sometimes Delphi may 'automatically' trap certain types of exception. For example, if you pass a string to the `StrToInt` function and the conversion fails, Delphi may show an error message. This only works, however, if a specific compiler option is set (the *I/O Checking* option must be enabled by selecting the *Project* menu, then *Options* and in the dialog box finding *Delphi Compiler/Compiling* then locating *Runtime Errors* and making sure a tick appears alongside *I/O Checking*. However, even built-in exception handling doesn't trap all exceptions and it doesn't give you the ability to control exactly what happens in your code when an exception occurs. So don't rely upon it!

Exceptions

It is up to the programmer to trap exception objects and recover from errors so that the program can continue executing. If this were not done, the program would (at best) be left in an uncertain state and might (at worst) crash.

In order to handle an exception, you need to enclose and thereby 'protect' the hazardous piece of code (here the `StrToInt` conversion) between the keywords `try` and `except`. This is how this has been done in the `LoadBtnClick` procedure:

cddbase

```
try
    recNum := StrToInt(RecNumEd.Text);
except
```

Following the keyword `except` you can write a block of code to be run if an exception occurs. Typically this code may display an error message and reset any values which might have been corrupted by the code within the protected block. In this case, the value of `recNum` will be unpredictable if an exception occurs so it needs to be set to a valid integer, such as 0. The exception-handling code is placed between the keywords `except` and `end`. This is my code:

```
except
    on EConvertError do
    begin
        recNum := 0;
        MessageDlg('I''m terribly sorry but "' + RecNumEd.Text +
            '" is not a valid integer!',
          mtInformation, [mbOk], 0);
        invalidNumber := true;
    end
end;
```

This error message is displayed when the user enters 'xxx' as the record number:

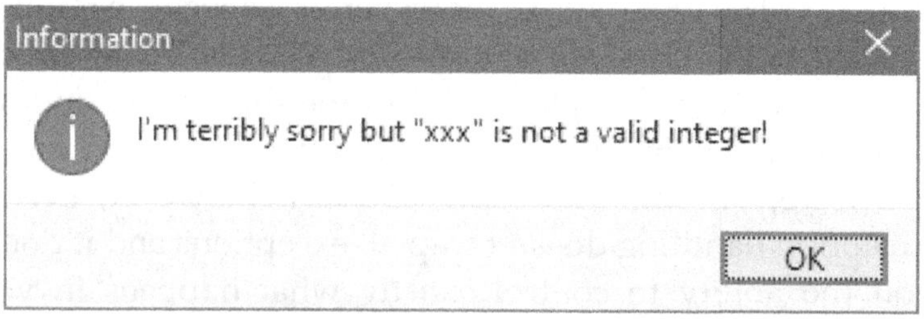

In my code, the test on EConvertError is optional. It provides a way of verifying that the exception here is of the type I think it is – namely an exception caused by a data-conversion error. Notice that I have also set a Boolean variable, invalidNumber, to true. The value of this variable is used to indicate to code later in the procedure that an exception has occurred.

Multiple Exception Types

In cases where more than one type of exception might occur it is possible to have multiple exception-recovery sections, each of which is designed to handle an exception of a particular type. The *convex* project provides a few examples of this.

Let's suppose, for example, that you have some code that tries to convert a string to an integer. This might happen if the user enters an alphabetic character into a text box when an integer was expected. The code show below deliberately creates this sort of error and shows a message when the exception is trapped:

convex

```
try
    StrToInt('a');
except
    ShowMessage('There''s been a problem!');
end;
```

Run Without Debugging

Delphi (and Lazarus) may display its own exception-handling dialog prior to your message being shown. In Delphi this only appears when debugging (select *Run Without Debugging* to avoid these dialogs). In Lazarus, you may disable debugging dialogs by clicking *'Ignore this exception type'* when the dialog first appears.

In fact, when trying to convert user input, there are also other sorts of exception that might occur. If, for example, someone were to enter 0 and an attempt were then made to divide by that number, an EZeroDivide exception would occur rather than an EConvertError.

The *convex* sample project shows how the same exception-handling block can deal with multiple exception types by adding multiple on *<Exception>* do handler sections. If you do this in your own code you should be sure to place the most *specific* exception types first and the most *generic* types last. If you were to place a generic handler to deal with the base `Exception` type first then that would always be executed since all exceptions are compatible with the `Exception` class. But if you put this *generic* `Exception` handler right at the end it will only execute when one of the more *specific* exception-handlers has not already dealt with exceptions of the specified classes:

```
try
    // code that risks causing an error is placed here
except
    on EConvertError do
        ShowMessage('There''s been a conversion error');
    on EZeroDivide do
        ShowMessage('There''s been a zero divide error');
    on Exception do
       ShowMessage('There''s been an Exception!');
end;
```

You may optionally initialize an exception object by placing a variable before a colon and its exception type, like this:

```
on e: EConvertError do
```

You can then access information on the exception object. For example, an exception object has a `Message` property which provides a description of the error. Look at the following code:

```
try
    StrToInt('a');
except
    on e: Exception do
        ShowMessage('There''s been an Exception! ' + e.message);
end;
```

When this executes, this message dialog is shown:

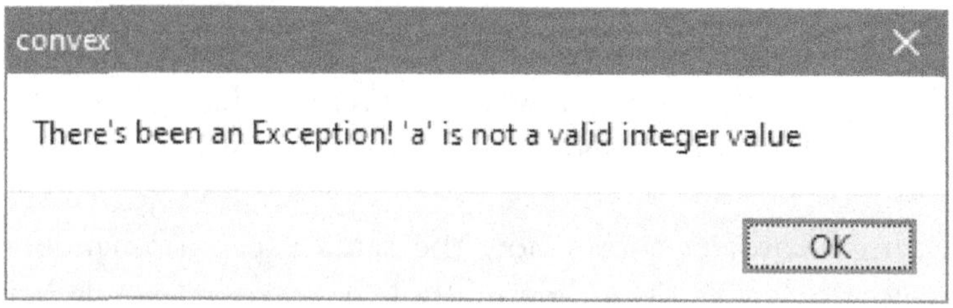

finally

Exception-handling blocks may also, optionally, contain a `finally` section. Any code in the `finally` section will run whether or not an exception occurred in the `try` section. So, for example, if you were writing data to a file, you might want to ensure that the file is closed whether or not an exception occurs. The `finally` section will take care of that:

```
var f : Text;
begin
    try
        Assign (f,'filename.txt');
        Rewrite (name);
        // process file contents here
    finally
        CloseFile(f);
    end;
end;
```

Debugging

Even the most careful programmer occasionally makes a mistake. In Delphi, the easiest way to spot an error is to use the integrated debugging tools. Load the project, *buggy*. This project is similar to the record-based CD database that we used earlier. But there's a problem. When you click the button, you'll see that it only displays nine CDs:

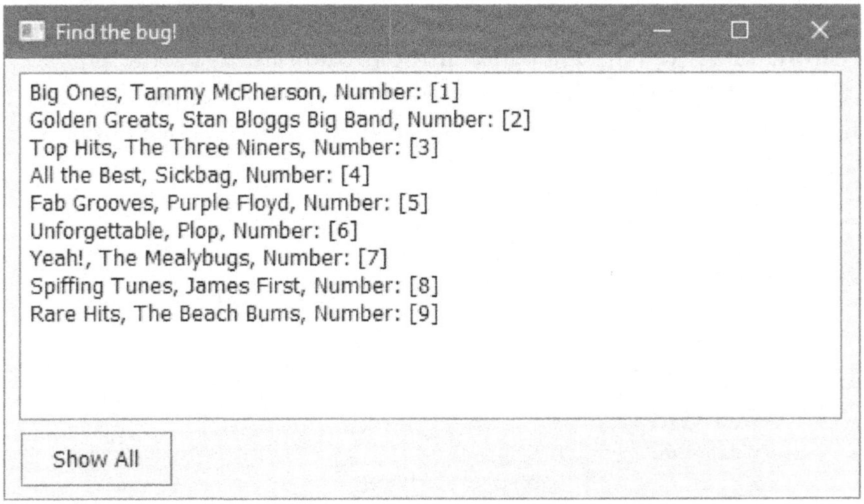

However, if you look at the code you'll see that the two arrays which initialize the records – `NAMEARRAY` and `ARTISTARRAY` – contain ten strings each:

buggy

```
const
    NAMEARRAY: strArray = ('Greatest Hits', 'Big Ones', 'Golden Greats',
      'Top Hits', 'All the Best', 'Fab Grooves', 'Unforgettable', 'Yeah!',
      'Spiffing Tunes', 'Rare Hits');
    ARTISTARRAY: strArray = ('The Worms', 'Tammy McPherson',
      'Stan Bloggs Big Band', 'The Three Niners', 'Sickbag', 'Purple Floyd',
      'Plop', 'The Mealybugs', 'James First', 'The Beach Bums');
```

The first record, which should have been initialized with the name 'Greatest Hits' by 'The Worms', has gone missing. Let's see if we can find where it's gone. Find the `TForm1.ShowAllBtnClick` procedure. Now find the line beginning `Memo1.Lines.add` and click in the left-hand margin of the editor. The entire line will be highlighted and a breakpoint marker (a red circle) will appear in the margin. This shows that a 'breakpoint' has been placed on this line:

```
    aCD := obArray[i];
    Memo1.Lines.add(aCD.name {  *** place a breakpoint on this line! *** }
      + ', ' + aCD.artist + ', Number: [' + IntToStr(aCD.number) + ']')
end;
```

Now let's watch the value of the `aCD` variable. Highlight the variable name, `aCD` and press `[CTRL][F5]` or right-click and select the menu item: *Debug, Add Watch At Cursor*. You should now see a *Watch List* window stating: *aCD [process not accessible]*. Position the windows on screen to ensure that the *Watch List* remains visible.

Run the program in the debugger (`[F9]` or *Run* from the *Run* menu) and click the '*Show All*' button. The program will pause at the breakpoint. Now the *Watch List* window shows the data with which `aCD` has been initialized. This demonstrates that the record number 1 has been initialized with the data we'd intended for record number 2:

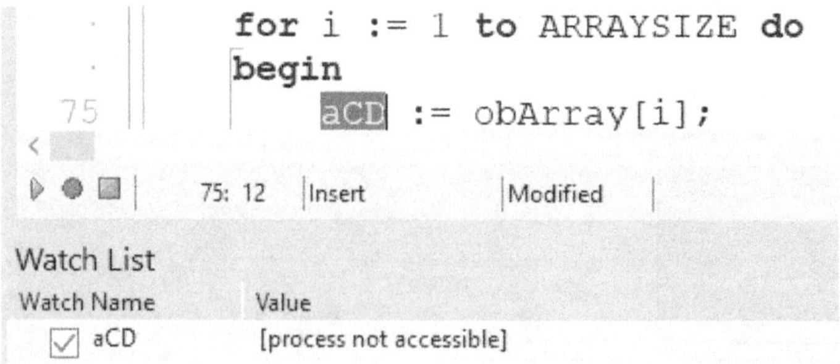

Display The Watch List

The window layout of Delphi may change when you start debugging. If the *Watch List* vanishes, you can make it appear again by selecting the *View* menu then *Debug Windows/Watches*.

You can watch the remaining records being initialized by continuing to run the program (`[F9]`) or by tracing through the code one line at a time (`[F7]`).

This test has established that the array 'slots' from 1 to 9 are all initialized. But the disappearance of the first record is still a mystery. Let's check the value of the `ARRAYSIZE` constant. Hover your mouse over `ARRAYSIZE` in the code. A tooltip shows you its value. You'll find that `ARRAYSIZE` equals 9. But, wait a minute, I'd thought this was a 10-element array!

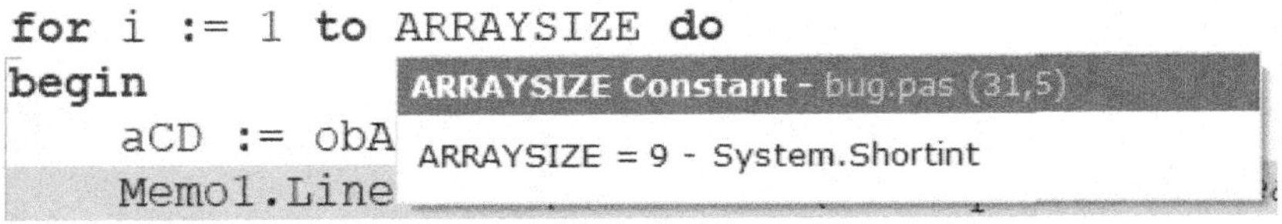

Scroll back to the `const` section near top of the code unit. This is the declaration of the `ARRAYSIZE` constant:

```
const
    ARRAYSIZE = 9;
```

In this program, the arrays are zero-based:

```
strArray = array [0 .. ARRAYSIZE] of string[20];
obArray: array [0 .. ARRAYSIZE] of CDOb;
```

They can indeed contain ten elements. But the array indexes are numbered from 0 to 9, *not* from 1 to 10. Which means that the apparently missing record has probably been in the array all along, hiding in slot 0. To check this, make sure you are running in the debugger and you are paused at the breakpoint entered previously. Now pop up the *Evaluate/Modify* dialog (press `[CTRL][F7]`) and, in the *Expression* field enter `obArray[0]`. Then click *Evaluate*. Sure enough, there's the missing record: `('Greatest Hits', 'The Worms', 0)`.

You may want to make sure that the last record (at index 9) is also found in `obArray`. Evaluate this expression:

```
obArray[9]
```

Sure enough, the *Evaluate/Modify* dialog shows that this record is in the array too:

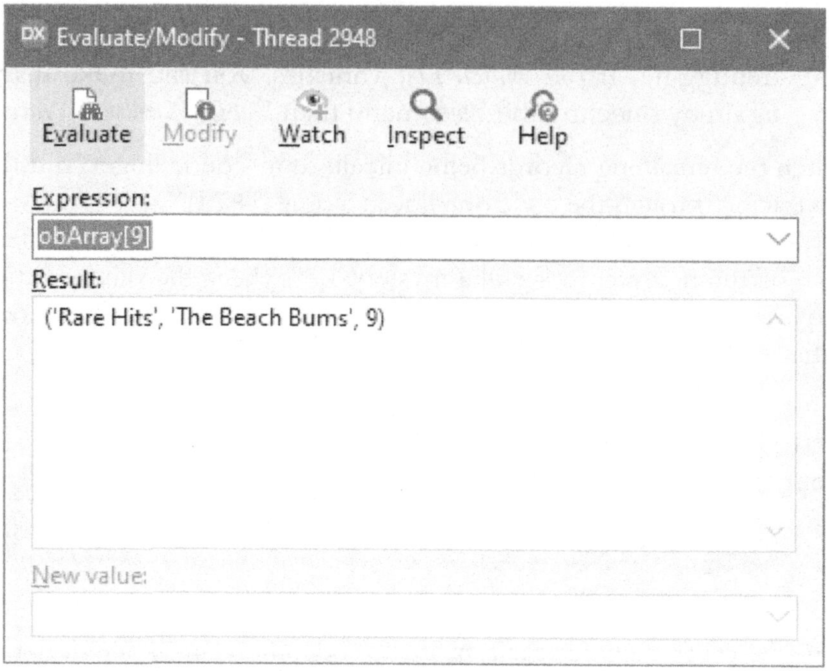

This shows that the array has been correctly initialized with all ten records, from 0 to `ARRAYSIZE`. The code in `TForm1.FormCreate` does that:

```
for i := 0 to ARRAYSIZE do
begin
    cd := CDOb.Create;
    cd.name := NAMEARRAY[i];
    cd.artist := ARTISTARRAY[i];
    cd.number := i;
    obArray[i] := cd;
end;
```

So I conclude that the error must be in the procedure responsible for *displaying* the data. Scroll down to `ShowAllBtnClick` again. And there's the problem! The `for` loop uses this expression:

```
for i := 1 to ARRAYSIZE
```

In other words, I initialized the array from 0 to `ARRAYSIZE` but I displayed the array elements from 1 to `ARRAYSIZE`, which missed out the array element at index 0. This is easily fixed. In `TForm1.ShowAllBtnClick` I just change the 1 to 0:

```
for i := 0 to ARRAYSIZE do
begin
    aCD := obArray[i];
    Memo1.Lines.add(aCD.name + ', ' +  aCD.artist + ', Number: [' +
        IntToStr(aCD.number) + ']')
end;
```

Now when I run the program and click the button, all ten records are displayed. Another bug bites the dust:

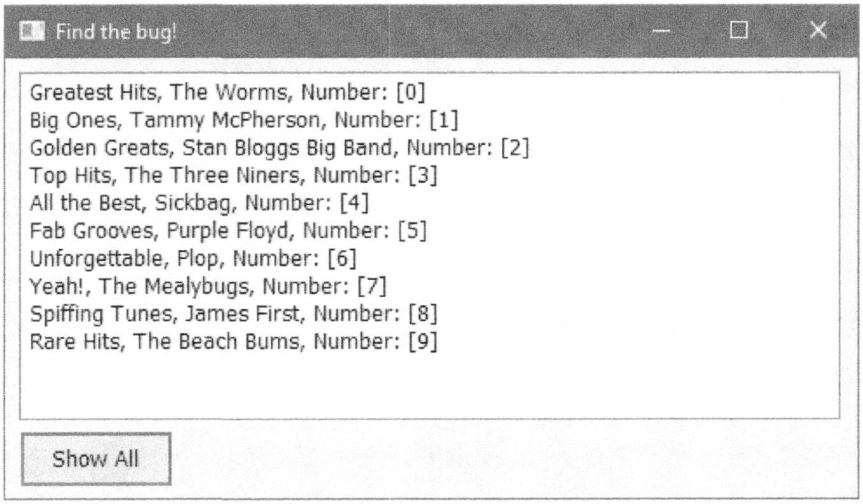

The Delphi Debugger

The debugging example given in this chapter shows only the basic features of the Delphi debugger. More detailed information can be found in the Delphi Help system. Press `F1` then, in the Index search box, enter: *overview of debugging*.

Chapter 10 – The Adventure Continues

This final chapter is not devoted to a specific programming topic. Instead, it provides an example of how to write and structure a more complex program than we have seen so far.

In this chapter I'll show how I went about writing a program that uses multiple classes saved in several code units. This program uses many of the techniques we've used previously and it also introduces some new features – in particular, the ability to save and load (that is to 'serialize') a complex network of objects to and from disk.

The program described in this chapter is an adventure game. It is a text-based exploring game in which the player enters commands to move from one location to another, collecting and dropping treasures along the way.

Adventure Game Programming

I have to confess that adventure games were responsible for getting me interested in programming in the first place. I started programming in the early 1980s shortly after IBM launched its first desktop PCs. I played some classic adventure games such as *'Zork'* and *'Starcross'*, became hooked and so I wrote my own game called *'The Golden Wombat Of Destiny'*. I still love adventure games and I think that writing one is a terrific programming project. If you want to learn the real secrets of adventure game programming, I have a book on that called *'The Little Book Of Adventure Game Programming'*. The main language used in that book is C#. However, its Appendix provides help on writing games in other languages with code examples in Ruby, Java and Object Pascal.

Not only are adventure games fun to play but they are also fun to write. What's more, they are a great way to increase your understanding of object orientation since all the items in a game – the rooms, maps, the player and the treasures – are naturally represented as objects.

The game project provided in the code archive for this book is called *wombat*. Load it into Delphi to look at its code. This game provides examples of many of the features of Object Pascal that we have discussed in this course. In the *advobs* unit, for example, you will find that I have created a hierarchy of related objects:

`ThingOb`	The class from which all other game classes descend.
`ThingHolderOb`	Which contains a `TList` of items, `_tlist`, to store the contents of rooms or the inventory of the game player.
`RoomOb`	A descendent of `ThingHolderOb` which adds on some exits (integers that will index into a list of rooms).
`ActorOb`	Which defines the player (and could be used for characters in the game) – this is a type of `ThingHolderOb` that also stores the character's position.
`MapOb`	A class with extra functions to return a `RoomOb` based on the room's index number, plus some methods to save and load data.
`Implementer`	The ultimate 'controller' of the game.

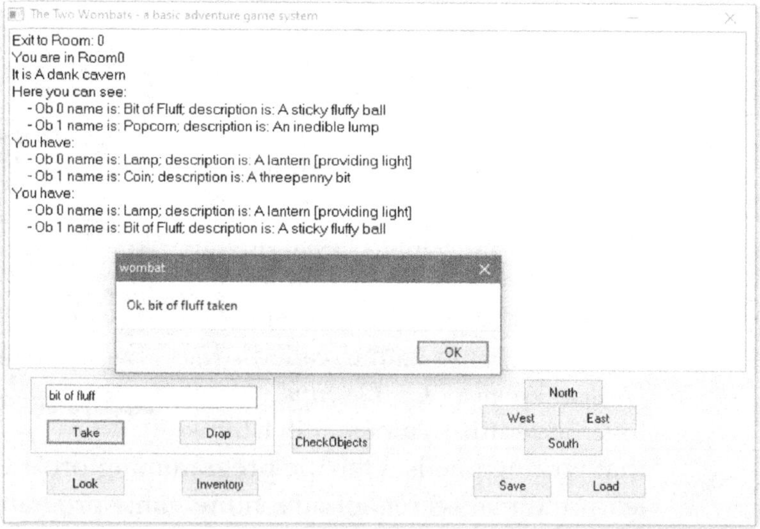

The sample game implements a map of rooms with exits into other rooms. You can click buttons to move North, South, West and East and you can enter the names of objects to take them (that is, to add them to your inventory) or to drop them in the current room.

One Unit Per Class

In a short and simple program like this one, it is reasonable to group together relatively small classes in a single unit. If your classes are more complex, however, it would be neater to have separate code unit for each class. The code archive provides an example of this in the *game02* project.

Using or 'Importing' Units

Notice that I've defined some constants in the interface section of the *AdvConsts* unit:

```
interface

const
    NOEXIT = -1;
    NORTH = 0;
    SOUTH = 1;
    WEST = 2;
    EAST = 3;
```

These constants can be 'imported' for use by other units by adding the imported unit name, `AdvConsts` to the comma-delimited list in the `uses` section at the top of the code file. This is how I have imported *AdvObs* and *AdvConsts* into *wombatmain.pas*:

```
uses
    Windows, Messages, SysUtils, Classes, Graphics, Controls, Forms, Dialogs,
    StdCtrls, ComCtrls, ExtCtrls, AdvObs, AdvConsts;
```

In a big project you would probably have many different source code files and you would need to import each by adding its name to the `uses` section when needed. I won't explain all the code in detail here. Having read this book, you should be able to understand it by reading it and running it. Use it as a revision aid. If there is anything in this project that you don't understand, refer back to the chapter in this book that deals with that topic.

Extend the Game

There are many ways in which my game can be changed, improved and extended. For example, consider whether the `SetPos` and `GetPos` methods of the `ActorOb` class might be replaced by a property:

wombat (advobs.pas)

```
procedure ActorOb.SetPos(num: integer);
begin
    _position := num;
end;

function ActorOb.GetPos: integer;
begin
    result := _position;
end;
```

Think about creating objects, such as treasure chests, that are able to contain other objects. Then consider what programming you would need to do in order to put an object into a container. And finally, try to think of puzzles have to be solved – how a locked door might be opened, how a maze might be implemented and so on. The fundamentals are all here to get you started. It's up to you how you develop it.

Saving Objects

There are objects of many types in this game, some of which may be modified as the game progresses. For example, the player's position may change and the list of treasures in each room may also change as they are taken and dropped by the player. This presents us with the problem of finding a way to writing all these objects to disk and reading them back into memory later on. This will be necessary to let the player save a game and reload it at a later date.

There is no easy way of saving the data of multiple object types to a typed file. A typed file works with a series of data items or records of the same size and structure. In a previous project (Chapter 7) I showed how to map each object onto a record and save the records to typed files.

But you can't save a mix of records to a single typed file, when some records have a `position` field (such an `Actor` object) while others which have four exits: `N`, `S`, `W`, `E` (`Room` objects). In order to save different types of records, I would need to create separate files to store the data for each type of record. That would be messy, awkward and inefficient.

Streams

There is an alternative. Object Pascal lets you save data of any type into 'streams'. A stream is a sequence of bytes, which are tiny chunks of information. Since all data of all types is made up of bytes, a stream is capable of storing mixed data of any type. The same stream can contain strings, integers, floating-point numbers and more complex data types.

There are several different types of stream available. The base type is the `TStream` class. Its descendant objects include `TMemoryStream` which writes to and from memory and `TFileStream` which writes to and from disk files. `TFileStream` is the most appropriate stream for our purposes.

Load up the *wombat* project and open the *advobs.pas* unit. This contains the definitions of the classes used in this game. The `Implementer` class is 'in control' of the game. One of its main features is to save and load game data. In the `SaveGame` function it creates a `TFileStream` object, `fs`, and then calls the `aMap` and the `player` objects' `WriteToStream` methods, passing to them the file stream object:

wombat (advobs.pas)

```
function Implementer.SaveGame(player: ActorOb; aMap: MapOb;
    aFileName: string): boolean;
var
    fs: TFileStream;
    ok: boolean;
begin
    ok := true;
    fs := TFileStream.Create(aFileName, fmCreate);
    try
        try
            aMap.WriteToStream(fs);
            player.WriteToStream(fs);
        except
            on Exception do
                ok := false;
        end;
    finally
        fs.Free;
    end;
    result := ok;
end;
```

Data is written to the `TFileStream` object using the `WriteBuffer` method. While there are several other data-writing methods available to stream objects, you will rarely, if ever, need to use them. The `WriteBuffer` method handles all normal types of data. The important thing to remember is that you must specify the number of bytes to be written as the second argument to the method as follows:

```
WriteBuffer(var buffer; sizeinbytes : Longint)
```

Find the `WriteToStream` procedure which I've written for my `ThingOb` class, which is the ancestor of the other classes in my game:

wombat (advobs.pas)

```
procedure ThingOb.WriteToStream(fs: TFileStream);
var
    currentClassName: shortstring;
begin
    currentClassName := self.classname;
    fs.WriteBuffer(currentClassName, sizeof(currentClassName));
    fs.WriteBuffer(_name, sizeof(_name));
    fs.WriteBuffer(_description, sizeof(_description));
end;
```

When a `RoomOb` or a `MapOb` or an `ActorOb` (such as the `player`) object needs to save its data to the stream, it is `ThingOb.WriteToStream` which executes first. This gets the name of the actual class, which might be 'RoomOb' or 'ThingOb', for example:

```
currentClassName := self.classname;
```

It writes this name into the stream using the `sizeof` function to ensure that the correct number of bytes are written to store the class name:

```
fs.WriteBuffer(currentClassName, sizeof(currentClassName));
```

Then it writes the object's internal data fields, again using `sizeof` to ensure that the correct number of bytes are written:

```
fs.WriteBuffer(_name, sizeof(_name));
fs.WriteBuffer(_description, sizeof(_description));
```

If you look at `RoomOb.WriteToStream`, you'll see that it calls `inherited WriteToStream(fs)` to ensure that `ThingOb.WriteToStream` is run first. Then it writes its own additional data fields to store the integer values of the four direction variables:

wombat (advobs.pas)

```
procedure RoomOb.WriteToStream(fs: TFileStream);
begin
    inherited WriteToStream(fs);
    fs.WriteBuffer(_n, sizeof(_n));
    fs.WriteBuffer(_s, sizeof(_s));
    fs.WriteBuffer(_w, sizeof(_w));
    fs.WriteBuffer(_e, sizeof(_e));
end;
```

An `ActorOb` object writes its data into a stream in a similar way. First it calls the inherited `WriteToStream` procedure which will cause its ancestor classes to write their data into the stream. Then it writes its position:

```
procedure ActorOb.WriteToStream(fs: TFileStream);
begin
    inherited WriteToStream(fs);
    fs.WriteBuffer(_position, sizeof(_position));
end;
```

Notice that `ActorOb`, `RoomOb` and `MapOb` all descend from `ThingHolderOb`. The `ThingHolderOb` class is used to maintain a list of objects. A map contains a list of room objects; a room may contain a list of treasures and an actor (here the player) may collect a list of treasures by taking them from rooms. Rather than program the list-management routines three times for map, room and player, I programmed then once in `ThingHolderOb` and then the `MapOb`, `RoomOb` and `ActorOb` classes inherit those capabilities.

So, for example, `MapOb` relies upon `ThingHolderOb.WriteToStream` of its ancestor class, `ThingHolderOb`, to save all the rooms it contains. Take some time to think about this as it is a core feature of how 'serialization' (the ability of a network of objects to store their data) actually works:

```
procedure ThingHolderOb.WriteToStream(fs: TFileStream);
var
    i: integer;
begin
    inherited WriteToStream(fs);
    fs.WriteBuffer(_things.Count, sizeof(_things.Count));
    for i := 0 to _things.Count - 1 do
        ThingOb(_things[i]).WriteToStream(fs);
end;
```

First of all this saves the number of items in the list, `_things.Count` – here, that's the number of rooms in the map. Then, for each item, it calls `WriteToStream` (inside a `for` loop), so that each item writes its own data into the stream. But `WriteToStream` is a *virtual* and *overridden* method. Remember (Chapter 8) that this means that the *specific version* of the method which is appropriate to each object will be called.

So if this is a `RoomOb` object, it is the `RoomOb.WriteToStream` method that will be called. If it is a `ThingOb` object, then it is the `ThingOb.WriteToStream` method that will be called, and so on. This means that even complex objects such as rooms that contain lists of things will be able to write their own data into the stream.

In principle, lists of lists of lists of objects will be able to write their own data. In a complete adventure game you might have a map containing numerous rooms containing a mix of monsters and treasures, with some of the treasures containing other treasures. The ability to save an entire network of mixed data types to a stream will be vital.

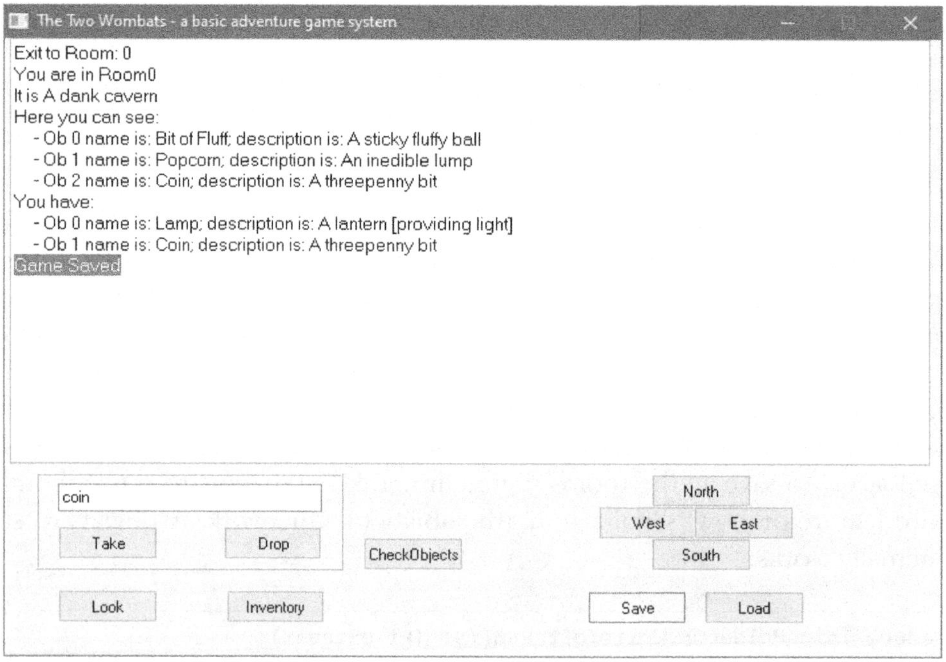

By writing data into streams, my game is able to save its current state – the position of the player, the treasures in each room, the treasures collected by the player and any other changes that have been made to objects in the game. Then the saved game can be restored later on to allow the player to start again from the place where they left off.

Loading Data

Having saved the game data, you have to be able to reload it and create from it all the objects needed to rebuild the game as it was when it was saved. This process begins in `Implementer.LoadGame`:

wombat (advobs.pas)

```
function Implementer.LoadGame(var player: ActorOb; var aMap: MapOb;
    aFileName: string): boolean;
var
    fs: TFileStream;
    ok: boolean;
    currentClassName: shortstring;
begin
    ok := true;
    fs := TFileStream.Create(aFileName, fmOpenRead);
    aMap.Free;
    aMap := MapOb.Create('Temp Map', 'Map prior to loading data');
    player.Free;
    player := ActorOb.Create('Temp ActorOb', 'A Temp Player', 0);
    try
        fs.ReadBuffer(currentClassName, sizeof(currentClassName));
        // read class name
        try
            aMap.ReadFromStream(fs);
            fs.ReadBuffer(currentClassName, sizeof(currentClassName));
            // read class name
            player.ReadFromStream(fs);
        except
            on Exception do
                ok := false;
        end;
    finally
        fs.Free;
    end;
    result := ok;
end;
```

This creates a file stream, `fs`, for reading, then it destroys the current map and player (`aMap.Free` and `player.Free`) and creates a new map and player. It then reads in the saved data.

The reconstruction of the game starts with a call to `aMap.ReadFromStream(fs)`. Once the map has been recreated the data of the saved player object is read in by calling `player.ReadFromStream(fs)`. These data-reading operations must be done in this order since the map and player objects were written to the stream (and saved into the file on disk) in this order. The data defining the map is restored by the `MapOb`'s ancestor `ThingHolderOb` in `ThingHolderOb.ReadFromStream`:

```
procedure ThingHolderOb.ReadFromStream(fs: TFileStream);
var
    i: integer;
    numthings: integer;
    currentClassName: shortstring;
begin
    inherited ReadFromStream(fs);
    fs.ReadBuffer(numthings, sizeof(numthings));
    _things := TList.Create; // remember to create a list here!
    for i := 0 to numthings - 1 do
    begin
        fs.ReadBuffer(currentClassName, sizeof(currentClassName));
        if currentClassName = 'ThingOb' then
            _things.Add(ThingOb.CreateFromStream(fs))
        else if currentClassName = 'ThingHolderOb' then
            _things.Add(ThingHolderOb.CreateFromStream(fs))
        else if currentClassName = 'RoomOb' then
            _things.Add(RoomOb.CreateFromStream(fs))
        else if currentClassName = 'ActorOb' then
            _things.Add(ActorOb.CreateFromStream(fs));
    end;
end;
```

This uses the `ReadBuffer` method to read in the data. Once again, it is the programmer's job to specify the number of bytes to be read. The `sizeof` function deals with this and it can be used either with a variable name or with the type of that variable. The two following statements, in which `n` is an integer variable, are equivalent:

```
fs.ReadBuffer(n, sizeof(n));
fs.ReadBuffer(n, sizeof(integer));
```

In my code I test the name of each class that is read in. Recall that this name was stored in the file prior to storing the data for each object. When I read back a class name it tells me how much and which type of data I can expect next. I then call the `CreateFromStream` method for each specific object type to recreate the objects.

Game Play Methods

One of the essential activities in an adventure game is the taking and dropping of objects. This is handled by the `TakeBtnClick` and `DropBtnClick` methods which you will find in the *wombatmain.pas* unit. These two methods work in similar ways. They transfer an object between one list and another – to or from the player and the room indicated by the player's position. Look at `TakeBtnClick`:

wombat (wombatmain.pas)

```
procedure TForm1.TakeBtnClick(Sender: TObject);
var
    thingsHere: TList;
    obName: string;
    ob: ThingOb;
    currRoom: RoomOb;
begin
    obName := inputEdit.text;
    currRoom := aMap.GetRoom(player.GetPos);
    ob := currRoom.ObInThings(obName);
    if obName = '' then
        ErrMsg('I don''t know what you want to take!')
    else if ob = nil then
        ErrMsg('There is no ' + obName + ' here!')
    else
    begin
        thingsHere := currRoom.GetThings;
        player.TakeObFrom(ob, thingsHere);
        ErrMsg('Ok. ' + obName + ' taken');
    end;
end;
```

This procedure begins by trying to find an object with the name (the `text` property) that the user has entered into the text box `inputEdit`. The `ThingHolderOb.ObInThings` function tries to match the name entered (`obName`) with the name of one of the items in the list of things which the specified object's list contains – for example, the items in the player's inventory or the treasures in a room. If the named object is found in the current room it is removed from the room's list and added to the player's list of things by the `TakeObFrom` method shown here:

```
procedure ThingHolderOb.TakeObFrom(var aThing: ThingOb; var tl: TList);
begin
    _things.Add(aThing);
    tl.Remove(aThing);
end;
```

As you can see, this procedure is incredibly simple. It uses the `Add` and `Remove` methods of the `TList` class (a standard Delphi class which `ThingHolderOb` uses to store a list of objects) to add an object to one list and delete it from another.

Moving Around the Map

Now that my player can take and drop objects, the next task is to let the player move around from place to place. The user interface of the game provides four direction buttons for this. In the Delphi form designer, double-click the *North* button to find `TForm1.NorthBtnClick`:

```
procedure TForm1.NorthBtnClick(Sender: TObject);
begin
    DisplayBox.lines.Clear;
    Display(imp.MoveTo(player, NORTH, aMap));
end;
```

Here `MoveTo` is a method of the `imp` object which is an instance of the `Implementer` class. The `imp` object is in overall control of the game. Other objects such as rooms, treasures and the player have full access to their own internal data and limited access to objects in their immediate vicinity – for example, when a player takes an object from the current room.

The `imp` object, on the other hand, has much greater access to the code of the entire game. I have already used `imp` to save and load all the objects in a game. Now I have also given it the power to move objects around the map much as a chess-player would move the pieces around a board.

In `NorthBtnClick` my code passes an `ActorOb` (`player`), a direction (`NORTH`) and a `MapOb` (`aMap`) as arguments to the `MoveTo` method of `imp`. To see what happens next, find the `Implementer.MoveTo` method in the *advobs* unit. This declares a set of parameters for the four arguments passed to it: `anActor`, `aDir` and `aMap`:

```
wombat (advobs.pas)

function Implementer.MoveTo(var anActor: ActorOb; aDir: integer;
    var aMap: MapOb): string;
var
    pos: integer;
    room: RoomOb;
    exit: integer;
    msg: string;
```

wombat (advobs.pas) [continued]

```
begin
    msg := 'Error: Oops! Cannot move there!'; // some unknown problem
    pos := anActor.GetPos;
    room := RoomOb(aMap._things.Items[pos]);
    case (aDir) of
        NORTH:
            exit := room.N;
        SOUTH:
            exit := room.S;
        WEST:
            exit := room.W;
        EAST:
            exit := room.E;
    else
        exit := NOEXIT;
    end;
    if exit = NOEXIT then
        msg := 'No Exit!'
    else
    begin
        anActor.SetPos(exit);
        msg := 'Exit to Room: ' + IntToStr(exit);
    end;
    result := msg;
end;
```

The code finds the current position of the player (the `anActor` parameter):

```
pos := anActor.getpos;
```

Then it retrieves the `RoomOb` at that position in the map:

```
r := RoomOb(aMap._things.Items[pos]);
```

A `case` statement is used to obtain the number of the room adjoining the current room in the direction specified. So if the direction is `NORTH`, the `RoomOb`'s `N` property returns the number of the room leading from the northern exit:

```
NORTH:
    exit := room.N;
```

Recall that the values of the directions constants such as `NORTH`, `SOUTH` and `NOEXIT` are defined in a separate unit, *advconsts*, which can be used by all other units that require access to those constants. Assuming that an exit has been located, the code then asks the actor object to alter its position to the index of the new room:

```
anActor.setpos(exit);
```

Finally, the `MoveTo` function returns a string stating the identity of the new room or 'No Exit!' if no exit was found in the specified location. This message is passed by the calling code (in `NorthBtnClick`) to the `Display` procedure in the *wombatmain* unit, which displays the string:

```
Display(imp.MoveTo(player, NORTH, aMap));
```

Now let's turn to the *Look* button. When clicked, this displays the name and description of the current room plus a list of the objects it contains:

```
procedure TForm1.LookBtnClick(Sender: TObject);
begin
    Display('You are in ' + aMap.GetRoom(player.GetPos).Name);
    Display('It is ' + aMap.GetRoom(player.GetPos).Description);
    Display('Here you can see: ');
    DisplayThings(aMap.GetRoom(player.GetPos).GetThings);
end;
```

The code in this procedure is straightforward. It establishes the player's current location, `player.getpos`, then it uses this value to retrieve the room object at that index in `aMap`. The `RoomOb`'s `Name` and `Description` properties are used to retrieve the values of its name and description variables:

```
aMap.getroom(player.getpos).Name
aMap.getroom(player.getpos).Description
```

For the purposes of testing and debugging, I've created a small map of six rooms, with just one `ActorOb` (the player) and a handful of treasures and assorted junk lying around in the rooms. The `imp` object is created and the `player` and `aMap` are initialized to the default value of `nil` beneath the `initialization` keyword (at the bottom of *wombatmain.pas*) which runs when the program is first run.

The `TForm1.CreateObs` procedure (which executes when the user interface is created after the game runs) calls `CreateObs` to create the actual objects (the 'treasures') as well as the rooms; it put the rooms into the map and it puts the treasures into the rooms or into the player's list of treasures.

Play the Game

If you haven't already done so, try playing this game now. In its present form it is too simple to be particularly entertaining. Even so, it illustrates the essential features of an exploring-style game.

Run it and click the *Look* button to see find out where you are. Then click the *Inventory* button to find out which objects you have. Now pick up an object. Enter *popcorn* into the edit box and click *Take*. Now click *Look* and *Inventory* again. You should see that the popcorn has been taken from the room and added to your inventory.

Now let's go exploring. Click *South*, *South* and *South* again. The third click will show you that you have entered a room with no exit to the south. Click *East*. You should now be in Room 5. Make sure that *popcorn* is still entered into the edit box. Click *Drop*. Now click *Inventory* and *Look*. You will find that you no longer have the popcorn which has been dropped in Room5. To save the game at this point, click *Save*.

Now, with *popcorn* in the edit box, click *Take*. Click *West* to move to Room4. Click *Look*. There is a wombat here. Enter *wombat* into the text box and click *Take*. Click *Inventory* to verify that you now have the lamp, the popcorn and the wombat.

Now restore the game you saved. Click *Load*. Click *Look* and *Inventory*. You should find that the game has been restored to its previous state. You are in Room5 again. The popcorn is back in this room and the only object you have in your inventory is the lamp.

What Next?

You are now at the end of this book. We have covered a great deal of ground and you should now be well-equipped with the knowledge to continue exploring Object Pascal development yourself. The best way to learn to program is to *do it*. Don't be afraid to take my sample projects and change them – add new features, improve existing ones. This is where the adventure begins. Now it's over to you. Good luck! I hope you enjoy your programming journey with Delphi and Object Pascal…

Appendix

This Appendix provides further explanation of a few topics mentioned only briefly in the main text of the book.

Free Pascal and Lazarus

Free Pascal is an open source, cross-platform Pascal compiler. Lazarus is a cross-platform IDE which can be used with Free Pascal. Free Pascal is broadly compatible with Delphi's Object Pascal. The design and debugging tools of Lazarus are similar (but not identical) to those in Delphi.

The Little Book Of Delphi provides no special support for Lazarus and Free Pascal and the code provided in the source code archive is not guaranteed to work with Lazarus and Free Pascal. Even so, in most cases the sample code should compile in Free Pascal. You may need to recreate projects and user interfaces in Lazarus, however. Download and install a version of Lazarus for your operating system here:

http://sourceforge.net/projects/lazarus/files/

For guidance on installation refer to these pages:

General Installation:
http://wiki.lazarus.freepascal.org/Installing_Lazarus

macOS Installation:
https://wiki.lazarus.freepascal.org/Installing_Lazarus_on_macOS

Anatomy of a Delphi Unit

A Delphi program may be made up of multiple *.pas* source code files called 'units'. A unit begins with the `unit` keyword followed by the unit name like this:

```
unit Age1;
```

This is followed by the `interface` keyword:

```
interface
```

The interface section contains declarations that are 'visible' to other units which use the current unit. These declarations may include constants, types, variables, procedures, and functions. This is a typical interface section for the main form of an application:

```
uses
    SysUtils, WinTypes, WinProcs, Messages, Classes, Graphics, Controls,
    Forms, Dialogs, StdCtrls;

type
    TForm1 = class(TForm)
    Button1: TButton;
    ScrollBar1: TScrollBar;
    Label1: TLabel;
    AgeLabel: TLabel;
    Label2: TLabel;
    Label3: TLabel;
    procedure Button1Click(Sender: TObject);
    procedure ScrollBar1Change(Sender: TObject);
private
    { Private declarations }
public
    { Public declarations }
end;

var
    Form1: TForm1;
```

The `uses` section is where other units that are required (those that need to be 'included') by the current unit are listed. In the example shown above, a number of 'standard' Delphi units such as `SysUtils` and `WinTypes` are used. These contain functions and procedures that are needed by code in the current unit. You may also list your own units in the `uses` section.

Then comes the `type` declarations. In the preceding example, the only type declared is the one that defines the form itself, `TForm1`. This includes the components such as buttons and labels, on the form, plus event-handler methods such as `Button1Click()`. The `TForm1` type definition is automatically written and updated by Delphi.

The `var` section here declares `Form1`, which is the variable name used to identify the main form of this application. You may also include your own publically accessible variables here. Following the interface section comes the implementation section. This begins with the `implementation` keyword:

```
implementation
```

The implementation section contains the actual code of the procedures and functions that have been declared in the interface section. Constants, types, variables, procedures, and functions can also be declared in this section in which case they will be private to the unit so (unlike declarations in the interface section), they won't be visible to other units. Here, for example, the implementation section contains the code of the two event-handler methods, `Button1Click()` and `ScrollBar1Change()` which were declared in the definition of `TForm1`:

```
procedure TForm1.Button1Click(Sender: TObject);
var
    age : Integer;
    teenager : Boolean;
begin
    age := ScrollBar1.Position;
    teenager := false;
    if (age > 12) and (age < 20) then
        teenager := true;
    if teenager then
        ShowMessage('You are a teenager.')
    else
        ShowMessage('You are no teenager!');
end;

procedure TForm1.ScrollBar1Change(Sender: TObject);
begin
    AgeLabel.Caption := IntToStr(ScrollBar1.Position);
end;
```

A unit ends with the keyword `end` followed by a full stop:

```
end.
```

This has been a somewhat simplified explanation of the anatomy of a typical Delphi unit. For a more detailed and complete explanation of Delphi units refer to Embarcadero's documentation:

http://docwiki.embarcadero.com/RADStudio/Rio/en/Programs_and_Units_(Delphi)

The Variant Type

While traditional Pascal is strongly typed and does not permit a variable declared as one type (say a string) to be assigned a value of any other type (such as an integer), Object Pascal also provides the option of declaring variables of the `Variant` type. This type is compatible with multiple other types. A variable declared to be `Variant` may be assigned integers, doubles, strings and other values like this:

```
var
    myVar : Variant;
begin
    myVar := 123;
    myVar := 10.5;
    myVar := 'Hello world ';
end;
```

Variants may be useful in special circumstances when the precise data type cannot be determined until the program is actually running. You should not use variants habitually, however; doing so will prevent your programs from being type-checked by the compiler and may introduce hard-to-find bugs into your code.

Constants

Delphi provides two varieties of constant: a *true* constant and a *typed* constant. True constants in Delphi cannot be changed. As we saw in Chapter 2, a constant is declared using the keyword, `const`.

True Constants

Constants are defined like this:

Consts

```
// These are constants - their values cannot be changed
const
    myConstStr = 'Hello world';
    myConstInt = 10;
    myConstDbl = 2.5;
```

Since the values cannot be changed, this is *not* permitted:

```
myConstStr := 'Goodbye Mars';
myConstInt := 25;
myConstDbl := 5.6;
```

You do not need to specify the *type* of a constant. In fact, if you do so, you will define *typed constants*, in which case you may be able to change their values in your code!

Typed Constants

This is how you would define typed constants:

```
// These are typed constants - their values can be changed
const
    myStr: String = 'Hello world';
    myInt: integer = 10;
    myDbl: double = 2.5;
```

In older versions of Delphi, assignable typed constants were allowed by default. In modern versions of Delphi, assignable typed constants are only allowed if a specific compiler option is enabled. If that option is enabled, this is allowed:

```
myStr := 'Goodbye Mars';
myInt := 25;
myDbl := 5.6;
```

To enable assignable typed constants in a project, select *Project*, *Options*, *Building*, *Delphi Compiler*, *Compiling*. Find *Syntax Options*, then the option *Assignable Typed Constants*. Set this to true or false to enable or disable the option Alternatively add the option `{$J+}` in the source code (as I have done in the *consts* project for Chapter 2) above the place in code where you want this option enabled. You may add `{$J-}` at a place in code where you want to disable the option later on. Assignable typed constants may be useful in some circumstances but they violate the expectation that a `const` cannot be changed so should be used with caution.

Naming Conventions

It's good practice to give descriptive names to your variables. However, there are a few things to bear in mind:

- Pascal is *not* case sensitive. A variable called `MyVar` can also be written `MYvar` or `myvar`. Other languages, such as C++, C#, Ruby and Java would treat these as three different variables.
- The first character in a variable name must be either a letter or an underscore. It must not be a number.
- The characters after the first letter may be letters, underscores or numbers.
- Variable names cannot include spaces or punctuation (such as dots, apostrophes or commas).
- You cannot use a keyword, such as `if`, `then` or `begin` as a variable name.

Example:

```
{ These variable names are valid }
MyVar
Start
Var23
Another_Var
_AnOKVar

{ These variable names are incorrect }
My Var
Begin
23Var
Another-Var
!AnIncorrectVar
```

When writing code you should try to adopt a set of 'naming conventions' so that your code looks neater and is easier to understand. There are no hard and fast rules on good naming conventions. The preferred conventions may vary from company to company, from programmer to programmer and from language to language. Some Object Pascal programmers follow the style guide employed by the programmers of Delphi. You can find that here:

http://www.sourceformat.com/coding-standard-delphi-borland.htm

Personally, I find some of these conventions a little peculiar (they don't conform to the way that I usually write programs) and therefore I do not slavishly follow the Delphi style guide. In particular, I don't like the convention of starting class names with a capital `T` (theoretically, this indicates that they are 'Types'), nor do I like the convention of beginning class variable names with the letter `F` (to show they are 'Fields').

A more common convention, across many different programming languages, is to give classes any name that you think is suitably descriptive and to write their names capitalized with a mix of upper and lowercase letters like this: `MyClassName`. This is called '*Pascal Case*' (or sometimes 'Infix Case') where every word in the identifier starts with a capital letter. For most variables and arguments, I begin the names in lowercase and include a mix of upper and lowercase letters like this: `myVarName`. This is called '*Camel Case*' For class variables and private variables I adopt the common convention of starting with an underscore and then giving the name in Camel Case like this: `_myClassVariable`.

If you are programming alone, it is up to you to adopt or define whichever naming convention you prefer. If you are a member of a programming team, the preferred convention will probably already be documented and you will be obliged to follow it. For an overview of the naming conventions used in this book, and those used by the programmers of Delphi, refer to the table below:

Identifier	This Book	Example	Delphi	Example
Variable	camelCase	`myVar`	PascalCase	`MyVar`
Argument	camelCase	`myArg`	PascalCase	`MyArg`
Class Variable	Underscore+camelCase	`_myClassVar`	F+PascalCase	`FMyClassVar`
Function	PascalCase	`MyFunction`	PascalCase	`MyFunction`
Class Name	PascalCase	`MyClass`	T+PascalCase	`TMyClass`
Constant	CAPS+Underscores	`MY_CONST`	PascalCase	`MyConst`
Keyword	lowercase	`begin`	lowercase	`begin`

More Sources of Information

There are many good online sources of Delphi and Object Pascal information. I recommend that you start with the following:

The Delphi Language Reference

The official guide to Delphi's Object Pascal:
http://docwiki.embarcadero.com/RADStudio/Rio/en/Delphi_Language_Reference

Delphi Basics

An excellent guide to Delphi with lots of short code samples:
http://www.delphibasics.co.uk/

Lazarus and Free Pascal Wiki

For cross-platform programming with Lazarus, start here:
https://wiki.lazarus.freepascal.org/

Object Pascal Video Course

The author of *The Little Book Of Delphi* also teaches a video-based Object Pascal programming course *Learn To Program Delphi & Object Pascal* using both Delphi and Lazarus. This course contains over 40 lessons and six hours of video instruction:
https://bitwisecourses.com/p/learn-to-program-pascal

Online Adventure Games

There are numerous adventure games that you can download or play online.

Infocom games can be downloaded, free, from several locations on the Internet such as http://www.infocom-if.org.

My game, *The Golden Wombat Of Destiny* can be played online or downloaded from: https://archive.org/details/TheGoldenWombatOfDestiny.

Other old adventure games are available from http://www.abandonia.com.

You may need a DOS emulator such as DOSBox http://www.dosbox.com/ to run some of these games.

Bitwise Books and Courses

For our full range of paperback books and eBooks plus free downloads, be sure to visit the **Bitwise Books** web site:
http://www.bitwisebooks.com

For video-based programming tutorials, go to the **Bitwise Courses** web site:
http://www.bitwisecourses.com

Visit the *Facebook* page of Bitwise Books & Courses:
https://www.facebook.com/BitwiseCourses

Subscribe to our *Twitter* feed:
https://twitter.com/bitwisecourses

There are lots of free lessons on the Bitwise Books *YouTube* channel:
https://www.youtube.com/bitwisecourses

Just One More Thing...

I hope you enjoyed reading *The Little Book Of Delphi*. As you end this book, I am already working on some a new books covering a range of programming topics. And you can help me! The one thing an author really needs is readers. And the most important way to attract new readers is to have reviews. That's where *you* come in.

I would be incredibly grateful if you could take a few moments to leave a short **review** of *The Little Book Of Delphi* on Amazon. Thanks in advance to anyone who leaves a review. You have no idea how much that means to me!

Good luck in your future programming with Delphi and Object Pascal.

Huw

Little Books Of ...

The Little Book Of Delphi is one of a series of '*Little Books Of*...' for programmers. In each *Little Book* we aim to give you *just the stuff you really need* to get straight to the heart of the matter without all the fluff and padding.

We know that there is plenty of information online about standard code libraries, so we don't fill the pages of these books by duplicating that information. Instead, we aim to explain the really important details that you need to gain a solid understanding of each subject and start hands-on programming as quickly as possible.

Some other '*Little Books Of* ...' are:

<table>
<tr>
<td>

</td>
<td>
<u>The Little Book of Adventure Games</u>
Writing Interactive Fiction games:
<ul>
<li>Create a map of linked 'rooms'</li>
<li>Moving around the map</li>
<li>Adding treasures to rooms</li>
<li>How to take and drop treasures</li>
<li>Putting objects into containers</li>
<li>How to save and load games</li>
<li>Most examples in C#</li>
</ul>
</td>
</tr>
<tr>
<td>

</td>
<td>
<u>The Little Book of Pointers</u>
An in-depth guide to pointers in C:
<ul>
<li>Indirection</li>
<li>Pointer arithmetic</li>
<li>Data Alignment</li>
<li>Linked Lists (single/double)</li>
<li>Stacks & Queues</li>
<li>Function Pointers</li>
<li>Common Pointer Problems</li>
</ul>
</td>
</tr>
</table>

	**The Little Book of C** A beginners guide to the C language: • Fundamentals of C • Variable & Types • Operators & Tests • Functions & Arguments • Arrays & Strings • Basic pointer operations • User-Defined Types
	**The Little Book of Recursion** Understanding recursion techniques: • Recursive Functions • The Call Stack • Stack Frames • Stack Corruption • Recursion & Scope • Tree Structures • Disk Directory Recursion
	**The Little Book of Ruby** A beginners guide to the Ruby Language: • Getting Started with Ruby • Object Orientation • Classes & Superclasses • Modules & Mixins • Methods & Arguments • Class & Instance Variables • Operators & Tests • Arrays & Hashes • File Operations • Exception-handling

You can also download a number of useful free resources from the Bitwise Books web site: http://www.bitwisebooks.com

Made in United States
North Haven, CT
12 November 2026

22198995R00109